"Why would you ever play if you don't want to be the best player who ever lived? That's how I think everyone would go into it. You want to be the man, you know, not the best of the moment, but the best who ever set foot on a basketball court."

—Kobe Bryant*

―――――――――――――

"Bryant is a prodigy in high-tops."
—*New York Times*

Philadelphia Inquirer

KOBE

THE STORY OF THE NBA's RISING YOUNG STAR
KOBE BRYANT

JOE LAYDEN

HarperPaperbacks
A Division of HarperCollinsPublishers

HarperPaperbacks
A Division of HarperCollins*Publishers*
195 Broadway, New York, NY 10007

ISBN 0-06-101377-3

HarperCollins®, ®, and HarperPaperbacks™ are trademarks of HarperCollins Publishers, Inc.

Cover photograph © 1998 Reuters/Scott Olson, Archive Photos. Back cover photo © 1998/Corbis-Bettmann

First paperback printing: October 1998

Printed in the United States of America

Visit HarperPaperbacks on the World Wide Web at
http://www.harpercollins.com

❖ 20 19 18 17 16 15

CONTENTS

So far, it had been a long night.

Kobe Bryant had made just one of five shots through the first three quarters. He seemed sluggish, a step slow. Maybe it had something to do with the back spasms he had experienced earlier in the week. Maybe it was the cumulative effect of a full season in the National Basketball Association, which can leave even the fittest athlete battered and bruised. Or perhaps he was simply straining beneath the weight of great expectations.

After all, in the previous two years Kobe had rushed at warp speed into the rarefied air of superstardom. In a single spring he had won a state high school championship, escorted a beautiful pop star to his senior prom, and become a first-round NBA draft pick. Sneaker deals and soda commercials soon followed. He had more money than he had ever imagined. And, of course, he had the opportunity to play basketball against his boyhood idols—men like Michael Jordan and Charles Barkley and Hakeem Olajuwon. It had all happened so fast. He was only nineteen years old, and already people were telling him that he was the game's savior. He would carry the NBA into the new millennium on his bony shoulders. With his broad smile and spectacular athletic ability, he was sure to be the next Jordan . . . the *Air Apparent.*

Kobe took all this in stride. He was nothing if not startlingly mature. Each night he went out and played as hard as he could. Everything else, he said, would take care of itself. For the most part, he was right. Kobe was one of the league's top rookies in the 1996–97 season. By the middle of the 1997–98 season, he was one of the league's top *players.* His popularity was soaring. Although he was not yet a starter for his own team, the Los Angeles Lakers, fans voted him to the starting lineup for the Western Conference at the 1998 All-Star Game in New York. Only Jordan played better than Kobe in that game. And no one was more entertaining. With an assortment of acrobatic dunks and long-range jump . shots, Kobe enthralled the crowd at Madison Square Garden. The kid was magnificent! Suddenly all the hype seemed perfectly appropriate.

The NBA season is long, however, and inevitably filled with twists and turns. Kobe felt the frustration of his first serious slump in late

February and March. Then came the sting of criticism from reporters and players who suggested that he had been anointed prematurely. Finally, he returned to All-Star form in the weeks leading up to the NBA playoffs. That, of course, was good news for the Lakers, who needed Kobe to be at his best if they were to have a chance for an NBA championship.

Now, though, it was the first night of the playoffs, and Kobe was struggling. So were the Lakers. Although they were heavy favorites to eliminate the Portland Trail Blazers in this first-round series, they found themselves trailing by three points early in the fourth quarter. The fans at the Great Western Forum were sitting on their hands, nervously waiting for an opportunity to erupt.

At that moment Kobe Bryant seemed like an unlikely candidate to provide the spark the Lakers needed. He had played tentatively throughout the game. In fact, he seemed almost nervous, as if the memory of the Lakers' final playoff game of 1997 was still on his mind. That one had ended badly, with Kobe tossing up several air balls in a loss to the Utah Jazz. Maybe he was worried about a repeat performance. Maybe he was . . . *scared?*

Maybe not.

Suddenly the ball was in Kobe's hands. He squared up far from the basket, some 25 feet away, and launched a three-point shot. The ball

rotated perfectly and landed softly, sweetly in the
bottom of the net. The score was tied, 80–80. As
the crowd at the Forum stood and roared, Kobe
balled his hand into a tight little fist. The
thinnest of smiles came to his lips.

It was now a brand-new game.

1

FAMILY MATTERS

*I*n the living room of his parents' neat suburban home, a three-year-old boy is acting out a fantasy. He puts on his San Diego Clippers uniform—a miniature replica of the one worn by his dad—and frantically dribbles a tiny foam basketball around the room. A bundle of energy and exuberance, he bounces off walls, crashes into furniture. All the while, though, he manages to keep an eye on a nearby television set. He can hear the announcers broadcasting the Clippers' game. He can see his father striding powerfully up the floor, then gliding toward the basket.

Before long the child's world intersects with the one on the screen. He, too, is airborne. He leaps at a small plastic hoop and slams the ball through. As the roar of the crowd crackles through the television's speakers, the boy pumps his fists in the air.

It goes on like that for the better part of two hours, the child copying what he sees on the *screen. He guards invisible opponents, swats away invisible shots, jukes invisible defenders. When Dad's team calls a time-out, the boy pulls up a chair, sips from a water bottle, and listens intently to an imaginary coach. He wipes the sweat from his brow with a towel bearing the Clippers logo, just like the big guys do. Just like Dad.*

When his mother enters the room, he looks up at her, wide-eyed. "Mom," he says. "I'm going to play in the NBA." She smiles and gives the boy a hug. She says nothing to discourage him, for she knows how fragile a dream can be. Especially the big dreams. As the game goes on, she watches the two of them, mirror images, father and son, and she thinks to herself . . .

Why not?

It has often been said that if you aspire to a career as a professional athlete, the smartest thing you can do is choose good parents. In just about every way imaginable, Kobe Bryant got lucky. He was born into a caring, loving family whose athletic roots ran deep.

His father, Joe Bryant, was a prep star who led John Bartram High School to the Philadelphia Public League basketball championship in 1972. Joe was recruited by some of the top Division I college programs in the country, including Maryland and Notre Dame. In the end, though, he decided to attend La Salle University in Philadelphia, so that he could remain close to friends and family.

While Joe was at La Salle, he began dating a young woman named Pam Cox. The two had first met while they were still in high school. Their grandparents lived on the same block, and occasionally the two teenagers would run into each other during family visits. Joe was captivated by Pam even then, and told some of his friends that one day he would marry her. But their romance would need a few years to blossom.

Interestingly enough, their first real date was preceded by a basketball game. Joe Bryant was playing for La Salle and Pam's brother, John "Chubby" Cox, was playing for Villanova. The two schools were both involved in a doubleheader one night at the Palestra, in downtown Philadelphia. Pam, a student at Clarion State, was in the stands to watch her brother play. But before the evening was over, she had turned her attention to Joe.

"I was sitting on one side and I see her parents, and she's sitting on the other side and sees my parents," Joe Bryant recalled during an interview with the *Philadelphia Inquirer*. "And I was walking around to see her parents, and she was walking around to see mine. It was kind of like a Miss Piggy and [Kermit the Frog] kind of thing: 'Hey, how you doing?' That type of thing. That night we went out on our first date."

Seven months later, Joe Bryant married Pam Cox. In the spring of 1975, after his junior year at La Salle, Joe decided to leave school and play professional basketball. In the 1990s, student-athletes commonly make this decision. In fact, in recent years the majority of players selected in the first round of the NBA draft have been underclassmen. But times were different in the 1970s. In order to enter the NBA before his college eligibility had expired, a player had to prove financial hardship. For Joe it wasn't difficult. He was a married man with a child on the way. His family needed the money.

There was no shortage of NBA teams willing to give Joe a job. After all, he was a lanky, 6-foot–9, 200-pound forward with the sensibilities of a playmaking guard. The Golden State Warriors drafted him in the first round, but Joe wanted more money than the team was willing to pay him. His tough negotiating stance was a gamble, but it worked out well. The Warriors traded Joe to the Philadelphia 76ers, who offered him a five-year contract worth nearly a million dollars. In today's NBA—where the *average* salary is more than a million dollars . . . *per year!*—that would be a laughably small contract. But in 1975 it was a staggering amount of money. And, as a bonus, Joe and Pam would get to stay in Philadelphia. He would play professional basketball in his hometown, and their children would be surrounded by family: aunts, uncles, cousins, grandparents. To Joe it was a dream come true.

• ● • ● •

Unfortunately, Joe's NBA career was not quite what he hoped it would be, in part because he did not fit easily into the role typically assigned to players his size. He was a flamboyant player who preferred dribbling and shooting to rebounding. Often he would stray far from the basket, into that area of the court usually reserved for guards. He liked making flashy moves and behind-the-back passes. Del Harris, who now coaches Kobe in Los Angeles, also coached Joe for a while in the early 1980s. According to Harris, Joe Bryant was ahead of his time. "Joe could do just about anything with a basketball," Harris once told a reporter. "He had about as good passing skills as anyone who played at that time other than Magic Johnson."

Joe was stylish off the court as well. In the heyday of disco, he often wore platform shoes, berets, and colorful silk shirts. He sometimes conducted interviews while puffing on a cigarette and pretending to play an imaginary guitar. He acquired the nickname "Jelly Bean" simply because of his fondness for candy, and because a fan once presented him with some jelly beans; to some observers, though, the nickname reflected Joe's carefree attitude. It was true that he could handle the ball better than most big men, and he had a nice shooting touch. In both areas, though, he needed improvement if he was to become one of the league's premier players. Quick with a joke and popular with the media, Joe sometimes seemed more concerned with promoting himself than with becoming the best basketball player he could become. "His lack of attention to detail prevented him from having a better NBA career," Jerry West, the Lakers' vice president of basketball operations, told the *Philadelphia Inquirer.* "Joe didn't want to play. He wanted to style."

Joe Bryant bounced around the NBA for eight years. He spent four seasons with Philadelphia, three with San Diego, and one with the Houston Rockets. Statistically speaking, his best season was 1980–81, when he averaged 11.6 points and 5.4 rebounds for the Clippers. Perhaps the most memorable, though, was 1976–77, when he was a defensive specialist for a powerful Philadelphia team led by Hall of Famer Julius Erving. The 76ers reached the NBA finals that year before losing in six games to Bill Walton and the Portland Trail Blazers.

By the spring of 1984, Joe Bryant's NBA career was over. But at only thirty years of age, he wasn't nearly ready for retirement. He was strong and healthy and still quite capable of playing ball. Surely, he thought, there was a team somewhere that could use his services. There were, in fact, many potential employers. None of them, however, was located in the United States. If Joe wanted to continue playing professional basketball, he would have to travel overseas, where American players—especially those with NBA experience—were highly valued. He could earn a good living in Europe. He could save some money and provide for his family while doing what he loved best. It wouldn't be easy, of course. American basketball players often experienced culture shock and homesickness when they arrived in a foreign country. Everything would be different for Joe: the food, the language, the people . . . even the sport itself. European teams usually played only one game a week and practiced twice a day. The rules of the game were different, too. And the crowds could be much nastier.

Joe talked it over with Pam. Together they decided to embark on the adventure of their lives. That summer they moved to Rieti, Italy, with three small children in tow: eight-year-old Sharia, seven-year-old Shaya, and their little brother—the baby of the family—six-year-old Kobe.

Kobe Bryant was born on August 23, 1978. His parents named him after a type of steak commonly found in Japanese restaurants, simply because they liked the way it sounded. It was a unique name for a unique child.

Kobe began watching his father's basketball games and copying his favorite moves when he was barely old enough to walk. By the time he was in elementary school, it was apparent that he was not only physically gifted, he was also an extraordinarily imaginative child. As Joe once told a reporter from the *Charlotte Observer*, "Kobe has always been a very creative young man. I saw him jump off a gymnastic springboard to propel himself for a reverse dunk when he was eight years old. That's when I knew he'd be special . . . different, whether it was basketball, football, soccer, or whatever."

Both father and son hoped it would be basketball, of course. As Kobe once told *Slam* magazine, "From day one, I was dribbling. I just found basketball to be the most fun. It wasn't just watching my father play. It was the fact that you could dribble the ball around everywhere. You could play the game by yourself and envision certain situations."

Basketball was primarily a solitary pursuit for Kobe. In Italy, as in most European countries, children grow up playing soccer, not basketball or baseball or football. So Kobe often found himself all alone on the basketball court. He'd watch videotapes of NBA games, then rush off to practice the moves he had seen. Sometimes he would pretend he was one of his favorite players: Magic Johnson, Larry Bird, Michael Jordan. Sometimes he would play a game he called "shadow ball," in which he'd try to beat the only opponent he could find: himself.

When other kids did show up on the basketball court, it was usually because they wanted to use the space to play soccer. "I could hold them off if there were two or three of them," Kobe recalled during an interview with *Sports Illustrated*. "But when they got to be eleven or twelve, I had to give up the court. It was either go home or be the goalkeeper."

Pam Bryant eventually bought a hoop for her son and put it up in the backyard so that he could play shadow ball without being interrupted. Adapting to other aspects of European life, however, proved to be a bit more challenging. Soon after arriving in Italy, Kobe enrolled in first grade at a local elementary school. He was surrounded by children who spoke a language he had never heard. For a while he felt completely lost.

"It was difficult at first because I couldn't speak Italian," Kobe told *Sports Illustrated for Kids.* "So my two sisters and I got together after school to teach each other the words we had learned. I was able to speak Italian pretty well within a few months."

If there were some things about growing up in a foreign country that were hard, there were also many benefits. Because they were strangers in a strange land, the Bryants learned to depend on each other in ways that many American families never experience. The isolation they sometimes felt led to an extraordinary closeness that remains to this day. "Everywhere I went, I went with my sisters," Kobe told *Slam*. "That's the reason our whole family is so tight now—we had each other's back."

In time the Bryants began to feel quite comfortable in Italy. In eight years Joe played for four different teams in four different cities. Wherever they moved, though, the Bryants found the natives to be warm and friendly. They also admired the obvious importance that Italians placed on the concept of family. "People treat others as equals there," Kobe once told a reporter from the *Philadelphia Inquirer*. "They don't mistrust each other. They say hello when they see you on the street. And family—family is big there."

Being exposed to such an intimate culture gave Kobe and his sisters a perspective on family they might never have experienced in the United States. As Joe Bryant told *Sports Illustrated*, "In America, families break apart because the son has to take a job in South Dakota. In Italy you'd see whole families living in one big villa. That's what our kids saw. We would go have a meal and end up sitting at the table, eating and talking, for three or four hours."

Despite the fact that basketball was a far less popular sport than soccer, Kobe found there were also athletic benefits to living in Italy. In the NBA, teams are on the road half the time. And when they're home, they typically practice in the morning hours. In Italy, though, travel is minimal, and at least one of Joe Bryant's daily practice sessions was in the afternoon, so Kobe frequently accompanied his father to the gym. As the team practiced at one end of the floor, Kobe would shoot silently in a corner. Every so often he would steal a glance at his dad and, just as he had when he was a toddler, try to copy one of his moves.

Joe Bryant was an extremely successful and popular player in Italy. He was a happy player, too, in part because his role was dramatically different from what it had been in the NBA. In Italy Joe was an offensive force, a scoring machine who routinely put up big numbers: 25 points, 30 points, sometimes more. He always seemed to have a smile on his face. Fans sang songs about Joe Bryant. They chanted his name during games and sought his autograph afterward. They loved him not only for his talent, but also for his exuberance. Both made an impact on young Kobe.

"My father always played with a great love for the game, and that's one thing he always taught me," Kobe once said. "He told me not to let the pressure or the expectations take away from my love for the game. I think that's the best advice anyone's ever given me. He taught me that you have to be a well-rounded basketball player."

Joe Bryant encouraged Kobe's artistry. He let his son know that it was okay to smile when he played, to express the joy he felt as he soared toward the basket. He wanted Kobe to be a stylish player, just as he had been. But, like any good parent, he wanted even more for his son than he had experienced himself. To that end, Joe Bryant taught his son the fundamentals of basketball: how to dribble with both hands, how to throw a clean pass, how to play defense, how to box out a defender when fighting for a rebound. He studied videotapes with Kobe. Together they would dissect the performances of some of the NBA's greatest players. Joe would give the remote control a workout—*play . . . pause. . . . rewind. . . . play*—as they memorized the flying dunks of Julius Erving, the no-look passes of Magic Johnson, the fadeaway jumpers of Hakeem Olajuwon. Before long Kobe possessed a devastating offensive arsenal. Sometimes he'd test his moves during games of one-on-one with Joe's Italian League teammates. By the time he was eleven, Kobe was winning some of those games.

On the occasions when he played pickup ball with kids his own age, of course, he dominated. Most of his classmates, though, were unimpressed. They didn't really care about basketball. They had neither the interest nor the ability to appreciate what they were seeing. "In Italy they told me, 'You're a great player over here, but when you get over to America, it won't be like that,'" Kobe recalled to *Sports Illustrated.*

He didn't listen to them. Even then, as a boy, he knew what he would accomplish. When he looked at the poster of Magic Johnson that hung on his bedroom wall, or when he watched videotapes of Michael Jordan, Kobe didn't see something that was out of his reach. He didn't see an impossible dream.

He saw his future.

2

HIGH SCHOOL ALL-AMERICAN

By the time the Bryants returned to the United States in 1991, Joe had saved enough money to take care of his family in fine style. They weren't rich, but they were comfortable. Eager to return to their roots, they naturally settled in the Philadelphia area—specifically, in a fashionably upscale suburb known as Lower Merion. Joe kept his hand in the sport by coaching junior varsity basketball at nearby Akiba Hebrew Academy, and by working as a consultant for local athletes who were training for the Maccabiah Games in Israel.

For Kobe and his sisters, the transition was a bit rockier. Even though they had spent portions of most summers in the States, they still suffered from culture shock. Their parents had given them tapes of *The Cosby Show* and videos by such pop music icons as Janet Jackson, and encouraged them to read biographies of Jackie Robinson and other prominent African Americans. Still, as an eighth-grader at Bala Cynwyd Junior High School, Kobe felt out of place. Not only was he a black student in a predominantly white school district, but he spoke English with an Italian accent. He didn't understand American slang. In just about every way imaginable, he was . . . *different.*

"It took a little while for me to get used to it," Kobe once said. "First of all, we didn't have to go to school on Saturdays anymore—in Italy, you have to go to school on Saturdays. So I was happy about that. But the size of the school—it was so much bigger. Plus, you had a lot more things that you could get into, whether it was negative or positive. There was a lot more risk when I came back over to America. Italy kind of sheltered me."

Even as a basketball player Kobe at first found acceptance hard to come by—particularly among his black classmates. As Pam Bryant told the *New York Times Magazine*, "They acted as if, if you weren't from the 'hood, you had no game."

Of course, Kobe did have a game. Even then, as a raw-boned thirteen-year-old, he had physical talents that could not be ignored, and before long word of his high-flying exploits reached the ears of Gregg Downer, the twenty-six-year-old varsity basketball coach at Lower Merion High School.

"I had heard all this talk about some out-standing eighth-grader," Downer recalled. "So one day we invited him to our gym, and he scrimmaged against our varsity. After about five minutes I turned to my assistant coach and said, 'This kid is a pro.' I knew right away, just by looking at his body and watching him play a little. Also, his father was standing in the corner, so I was aware that the kid obviously had good genes."

A former college basketball player, Downer had stayed in shape by competing in recreational leagues. After playing a few games of one-on-one with Kobe, though, he retired from competitive hoops. "I had to," Downer joked. "I couldn't beat a thirteen-year-old." The coach needn't have felt any shame. As it turned out, Kobe was no ordinary teenager. He was one of the most gifted and ambitious young athletes in the country, as everyone would soon discover.

When Kobe arrived at Lower Merion High School, he was expected to single-handedly transform the school's basketball team into some sort of juggernaut. But that would take time. In previous years the Aces had been only modestly competitive in the suburban Central League. At a school where soccer and lacrosse were the most popular sports, even the addition of Kobe Bryant would not be enough to suddenly ignite a run at a state championship. Not right away, anyway.

Lower Merion suffered through a long, hard

winter in the 1992–93 season, winning just three conference games and going 4–20 overall. There was, however, cause for optimism. The Aces were one of the youngest teams in the Central League, and their best player was just a freshman. Kobe led the Aces in scoring with an average of 18 points per game; he was also the team's top rebounder. Sometimes, even in the middle of a terrible loss, Kobe would throw down a spectacular dunk or deliver a perfect no-look pass that left coaches, spectators, and opponents wide-eyed with disbelief.

In those brief, startling moments, it was obvious that he was a very special player. In time, there would be no stopping him.

"I've seen a lot of high school basketball, but I have never seen anyone as good as Kobe was," Downer said. "He had such enormous potential. You could see that right away. He also had a great work ethic and a tremendous desire to succeed, which is something you don't often see in kids that age."

In the off-season Kobe pushed himself even harder. While other kids wasted time watching television or playing video games, Kobe concentrated on two things: schoolwork and basketball. He jogged almost every day, running for miles in his neighborhood until he thought he would collapse. He jumped rope. He lifted weights. He spent hours at a nearby playground, practicing his dunks on a 9-foot, 6-inch basket because it boosted his confidence and creativity.

In the summer after his freshman year, in addition to playing in some intensely competitive summer leagues, Kobe regularly played one-on-one with his father. Joe Bryant was nearly forty years old at the time, but he still had the size and strength—and the experience—to teach his son a thing or two. "He let me go by him once, then the next play he went right by me, stuffed it on me," Kobe told the *Philadelphia Inquirer*. "I didn't think he was that quick. He shocked me."

It was a valuable lesson for Kobe, since it made him realize that he still had a lot to learn about the game. It also reinforced what he heard so often when he went to the Spectrum to watch the 76ers play: that Joe Bryant also had a game. Father and son were already extraordinarily close, and there was no one Kobe respected more. But hearing others reminisce about "Jelly Bean" always brought a proud smile to Kobe's face.

"At Sixers games, all people ever tell me is that he was a great player," Kobe said at the time. "I love it. Whenever I step on the court, I think of that, that my dad went through this and now I'm going through it."

Kobe tried to emulate his father not only in the way he played, but in his attitude as well. "Dad would always have a smile going, be very calm, but be very emotional. That's what I would like to be. You go out there, give a hundred and ten percent, and have fun."

Kobe, a 6-foot–5 guard, did exactly that in his sophomore season. He averaged a team-high 22 points and 10 rebounds per game as Lower Merion went from doormat to contender in the Central League. The Aces finished the season with a respectable 16–6 record—they even won a game in the District I playoffs. By then it was clear that Kobe Bryant was definitely the best schoolboy basketball player in Delaware County, and probably in the entire state of Pennsylvania; and that Lower Merion High School was about to become one of the most formidable programs in the state.

Kobe once explained his passion for basketball, and his insistence on training harder than anyone else around him, by saying, "Why would you even play if you didn't want to be the best player who ever lived? That's how I would think everyone would go into it. You want to be the man, you know, not the best of the moment, but the best who ever set foot on a basketball court."

With that in mind Kobe devoted the summer of 1994 almost exclusively to the pursuit of excellence in basketball. He played in no less than six leagues and attended two summer camps: the prestigious Adidas ABCD Camp at Fairleigh Dickinson University (he was one of only four juniors invited), and another at La Salle University, where his father had become an assistant coach. It wasn't unusual for Kobe to arrive at one of the downtown Philadelphia courts as early as nine A.M. and not leave until nine P.M. For hours on end he would work and run and sweat. The thought of injury or burnout never entered his mind. The basketball court, he often said, was the place where he was happiest. He couldn't imagine ever growing tired of the game.

In Ardmore, Pennsylvania, where Lower Merion High School is located, Kobe's enthusiasm was infectious. Basketball suddenly became the most popular sport in town. At the dawn of a new season, the Aces looked like contenders for the Central League championship. In addition to Kobe, who was now being touted as one of the top prospects in the country, Lower Merion had a pair of experienced point guards in seniors Evan Monsky and Guy Stewart, and a talented 6–3 junior forward named Jermaine Griffin, who was playing in his second season for the Aces after transferring from New York City. They also had 6–3 senior center Chris Lawson and 6–3 senior forward Jesse Fedderman, both of whom had the size and experience to give opponents trouble inside. And there was a promising six-foot freshman named Dan Pangrazio, an athletic kid who would bolster an already impressive transition game.

Without question, though, this was Kobe Bryant's team. On most nights he would not only be one of the tallest players on the court, but the best ball handler and shooter as well. He would be Lower Merion's first option on each possession. Opponents knew it, too, but there was little they could do to stop him.

"I saw some truly amazing things in the time that I coached Kobe," Downer said. "The people who were fortunate enough to be inside the gym became accustomed to some of the things that he did. But if someone else stopped by to watch one of our practices and saw three or four of his dunks—the kind we saw every day—it would make their heads spin. I kind of got used to it, but it was still fun. I'd find myself drawing up imaginary alley-oop plays in my head while I was driving around in my car. Wherever I went, I'd be thinking about different ways to utilize Kobe's athleticism, to get him the ball. He was incredible."

Although awestruck by his star player's gifts, Downer was shrewd enough as a coach to know that he could not simply let Kobe do whatever he wanted on the floor. Basketball is the ultimate team sport, and even the greatest players cannot win without help from their teammates. Michael Jordan won four NBA scoring titles in his first six years in the league, but it wasn't until the Bulls surrounded him with a talented supporting cast that he finally won a championship. Wilt Chamberlain averaged 50.4 points per game in the 1961–62 season—a record that no one has come close to breaking—but it wasn't enough to lead the Philadelphia Warriors to an NBA title. Even Shaquille O'Neal, the most dominant big man of the 1990s, couldn't carry the Orlando Magic to an NBA title on his sturdy shoulders. That's one reason he moved to Los Angeles, so that he'd be surrounded by talented players.

None of this was lost on Gregg Downer. Kobe was Lower Merion's go-to guy—no question about it. But he would be expected to get his teammates involved in the offense. If he began playing one-on-five, he'd have to take a seat on the bench.

"I think it was important that we still made an effort to play team ball," Downer said. "Kobe had an obligation to exercise good shot selection, just like every other kid on the team. There were times when he was taking what I considered to be bad shots, and he came out of the game, just like anybody else. It was important that the other kids saw that. It made us a better team.

"Fortunately, Kobe has a passer's mentality, which made it a lot easier. He did a good job of involving his teammates. A big part of our success in Kobe's last two years was that he would get double- and triple-teamed, and he would give it up. We had a couple of kids who could really stick the three. That's what made us so tough: opponents had to pick their poison. Do you want to give us an open three-point shot, or do you want to try to guard Kobe Bryant with one man?"

Expectations for the Aces were high heading into the 1994–95 season. To prepare his team for the rigors of post-season tournament competition, Downer strengthened the team's non-league schedule, adding several regional and national powerhouses, including St. Anthony's of Jersey City, New Jersey, which has produced NBA point guard Bobby Hurley, among others.

The preparation paid off. Lower Merion, which had lost nearly as many games as it had won in Downer's first four seasons, went 26–5 and reached the second round of the Class AAAA Pennsylvania state playoffs. Along the way the Aces captured the Central League title, clinching first place with a 76–70 victory over six-time defending champion Ridley behind Kobe's 42 points.

That performance was typical of the way Kobe played throughout the season. He averaged 31.1 points, 10.4 rebounds, 5.2 assists, 3.8 blocked shots, and 2.3 steals. On most nights Kobe was so impressive that he looked like a pro who had walked into the wrong gym. Opponents were powerless to stop him.

The Aces' remarkable season finally came to an end in late March, with a 64–59 loss to Hazelton. Kobe had 33 points and 15 rebounds in that game, but it wasn't enough. Afterward in the locker room, he stood up and apologized to his teammates for not doing even more. Choking back tears, Kobe promised to try even harder the next year, to do whatever was necessary to carry Lower Merion to a state championship.

The summer of 1995 was a whirlwind of activity for Kobe. As always, he worked out with an intensity that bordered on fanaticism. He practiced his outside shooting and dribbling for hours on end. He lifted weights and ran until he was fatigued. And, of course, he played games. The difference this summer was that Kobe was now widely regarded as one of the top schoolboy players in the nation. That status earned him invitations to all of the best camps and tournaments. In early July he returned to the Adidas ABCD Camp in Teaneck, New Jersey, where he was named most valuable player. A week later he flew to Las Vegas to compete in the Adidas Big-Time Tournament, which featured most of the country's blue-chip prospects. Then, at the end of August, Kobe led Delaware Valley to a first-place finish in the scholastic division of the Keystone State Games. In that tournament he averaged 38 points and was named MVP. In the title game he scored 47 points as Delaware Valley surprised Philadelphia, 104–99. Kobe's performance in that game was particularly impressive since it came against a coach who knew all of his strengths and weaknesses: Gregg Downer.

"I loved it, because it was just another challenge," Kobe told the *Philadelphia Inquirer.* "He knows my game, and I know he would try anything to stop me. Right before tip-off I went over and told him, 'I'm coming at you.' He knows he's going to hear about this for the rest of the year."

In truth, there was little Downer could do to stop Kobe. Keystone Games rules prohibit the use of zone defense or even double-teaming, so the Philadelphia team was forced to contend with Kobe on a man-to-man basis, which was hopeless. "Kobe is in a league of his own," Downer said afterward. "He just has levels of his game that no high school player has possibly ever reached, at least locally. With no double-teaming and no zones, what can you do? I don't think it's a secret that Kobe is unstoppable being covered by one guy."

Even when that guy was several years older and a lot more experienced. The true measure of Kobe's potential came not at summer camps or in tournaments, when he was playing against other kids, but in pickup games with some of the best athletes on the planet. It was shortly after his junior year when Kobe first received permission from John Lucas, who was then coach of the Philadelphia 76ers, to work out with his team. Kobe was a skinny sixteen-year-old at the time, but it didn't take long for him to prove that he could hold his own against NBA talent.

"There were rumblings that he was tearing up

Jerry Stackhouse in one-on-one games," Downer recalled. "I don't doubt it was true. I watched him play with the Sixers that summer, and he fit right in."

Kobe didn't deny that the stories were true. But in fairness to Stackhouse, an All-American from North Carolina who had been the third pick overall in the NBA draft just a few weeks earlier, there may have been an element of surprise at work. "They had all the coaches watching and so forth," Kobe told the *Los Angeles Times*. "I think I kind of took him by surprise, because he had no clue who I was. I got a letter from [North Carolina coach] Dean Smith two weeks later."

Word traveled quickly, all right. Pretty soon every Division I basketball program in the country was chasing Kobe. NBA scouts were starting to pay attention, too. As the weeks went by, and the 76ers grew accustomed to watching Kobe play, he stopped being a novelty act and became a legitimate pro prospect. He may have been sixteen years old, but he had the talent and ambition of an NBA superstar. No one had ever seen anything quite like it.

"He has great court savvy," 76ers forward Sharone Wright told the *Philadelphia Inquirer*.

"He loves to put the ball in the basket. He has great moves. He can shoot. He can jump out of the gym."

Perhaps the greatest compliment paid to Kobe that summer, though, was when the invitations became less frequent. As Fred Carter, a former 76ers coach, told the *Philadelphia Inquirer Magazine*, "The buzz I heard was that Kobe was kicking so much butt in there that some days they had to get him out of the gym. He was demoralizing guys."

By the time fall rolled around and high school basketball practice began, Kobe Bryant had become the most highly recruited player in the nation. The list of schools pursuing him included many of the most successful programs in the NCAA: Duke, Michigan, Kentucky, North Carolina, Arkansas. And, of course, La Salle, which had Joe Bryant as its most formidable weapon in the recruiting war. By now, though, rumors were swirling around that Kobe might not attend college at all. If he was capable of playing with pros at sixteen, surely he'd be ready for the NBA at eighteen.

Right?

For his part, Kobe wasn't talking. He had other things on his mind, like a state high school championship.

The winter of 1995–96 was unlike anything Lower Merion High School had ever experienced. It began with great expectations, the promise of another run at a state title, and the belief that anything less would somehow constitute failure. That might have been unfair, but it was nonetheless understandable. Kobe Bryant was the backbone of the team, of course. Already one of the most physically impressive players in the country, he'd grown an inch (to 6–6) and added 15 pounds of muscle to his lean frame. He was healthy and hungry. It seemed like nothing could stop him.

Compounding matters for Lower Merion's opponents was the fact that Kobe was not a one-man team. Jermaine Griffin was back to provide strength inside. Dan Pangrazio had sharpened his shooting skills, giving the Aces another outside scoring threat and making it even riskier to double-team Kobe. Indeed, Lower Merion seemed to be a complete team, one which had all the ingredients necessary to win a state championship. All of which must have had Gregg Downer scratching his head in late December, as he watched his talented team lose three of its first seven games.

The low point came at the Beach Ball Classic in Myrtle Beach, South Carolina, where the Aces dropped an overtime decision to Jenks High School of Oklahoma. Lower Merion played selfishly and badly in that game, and afterward Downer was so upset that he gathered his players together in a hotel room and delivered a stern lecture. He chastised them for putting individual goals ahead of team goals, and for failing to accept their roles. He reminded them that their success in the previous season had stemmed not just from talent but from unity. In no uncertain terms Downer spelled out the rules for the remainder of the season. Each player would have a clearly defined role and limitations within that role. Some players, in other words, would be allowed to shoot the ball from 20 feet away from the basket; others would barely be allowed to shoot at all. His message was harsh but necessary. And there would be no discussions. If anyone couldn't accept his role, Downer said, he could turn in his uniform.

Immediately.

No one did. Instead, the Aces put their egos aside for the good of the team. That, as it turned out, was the pivotal point in a remarkable season. Lower Merion went on to win 27 consecutive games and the school's first state basketball championship since 1943. A team that only a few years earlier had trouble drawing anyone to its games suddenly became the hottest ticket in southeastern Pennsylvania. Scalpers routinely asked for—and received—as much as *a hundred dollars* for a ticket to a Lower Merion game! Autograph hounds would clog the hallway leading to the team's locker room, praying that Kobe would stop and share a moment or two with his fans—which he usually did. Each game was a spectacle, and Kobe was at its core.

"The environment was electric," Downer recalled. "It was so alive, especially during our state title run. There were long lines waiting for

tickets, cameras everywhere, national news people coming into our place on a daily basis,
phones ringing off the hook. Kobe handled it all
well. He was very mature, very accommodating,
but it got to the point where I had to hire a public relations guy to take the heat off him. It was
very exciting, though, playing in front of huge
crowds and all that. Traveling with Kobe was
like traveling with a rock star."

As the season progressed, Lower Merion
seemed to improve with each successive game.
For Kobe, jaw-dropping performances became
the norm. On January 25 he scored a career-high
50 points in 95–64 victory over Marple
Newtown. Lower Merion went on to win a second consecutive Central League title and earn a
number three seeding in the District I Class
AAAA playoffs. In the quarterfinals of that tournament, in his final home game, Kobe again
scored 50 points as the Aces rolled to a 95–68
victory over Academy Park.

Academy Park, the number 19 seed, made
the mistake of trying to run with Lower Merion.
The result, predictably, was a lopsided victory by
the Aces. After Academy Park scored the first
basket of the night, Lower Merion reeled off 12
unanswered points. By halftime the score was
45–25, and after three quarters the lead had
mushroomed to 28 points, 73–45. Kobe scored
his fiftieth point on a three-point jump shot with
a little over two minutes remaining. Moments

later, with the sellout crowd at Lower Merion gym giving him a standing ovation, he walked off the floor for the final time.

It was a touching moment for Kobe, who had brought so much excitement to the school and the community. "My career started in this locker room, in this gym," he said after the game. "The fans have shown their support. It's sad, but time goes on."

There wasn't much time for reflection. Lower Merion was on a mission, and several obstacles stood in the team's path. One of the first was Chester High School, which had whipped the Aces by a score of 77–50 in the District I title game a year earlier. When the two teams met again in March 1996, though, the Aces were prepared, mentally and physically. Each player wore the number 27 on his warm-up jersey to remind him of the margin of defeat the previous season. This time they would not be denied. Lower Merion captured the district championship with a 60–53 victory.

In the first round of the state tournament, Lower Merion got a scare from Cedar Cliff before rallying for the victory. In that game Kobe used the taunts of opposing fans to motivate himself and his teammates. And his coach.

"We were losing, and some of the fans from the other team were getting on us pretty good," Gregg Downer remembered. "They were chanting 'Overrated! Overrated!' It was a bit of a tense moment for us. We were down about eight points late in the first half, coming off a time-out, and we decided to use an orchestrated alley-oop play called 'special.' Sometimes we'd run it just to try to gain momentum, because it was such an exciting play—when it worked. This time our alley-oop passer threw kind of a bad pass, behind Kobe, but he went way up in the air and grabbed it with his left hand. Now, most players would be lucky to even catch a ball like that. But Kobe got it behind his ear with his left arm and just windmilled it down for a dunk. Our whole bench stood up and started pointing at the fans. It was wild.

"We went on a 12–0 run after that, and they never recovered. It was really an electrifying moment. At halftime I said to one of our assistant coaches, 'That's the best high school dunk I've ever seen.' And we were standing around silently for a minute, wondering whether that was an accurate statement, kind of downplaying it. But then someone said, 'Forget about high school. That's the best dunk I've ever seen—period!'"

A few weeks later the Aces ran into a familiar foe: Chester, which had qualified for the state tournament despite losing in the district tournament. The two teams met in the eastern finals of the Pennsylvania Class AAAA tournament on March 20 at the Palestra in Philadelphia. This time the game was even closer, largely because

Kobe, who was playing with a broken nose, got off to a poor start. The best high school player in the nation hit only eight of 25 shots in the first three quarters and turned the ball over five times.

Then he came to life.

Kobe scored 12 points in the fourth quarter and eight more in overtime as Lower Merion eliminated the Clippers, 77–69. His acrobatic shot in the lane with 2:02 left in overtime gave Lower Merion the lead for good, and his thunderous dunk with 14 seconds remaining brought the crowd at the Palestra to its feet.

"We knew it was going to be a war coming in," Kobe said. "We knew it would be a tough game."

Not the toughest, though. Three nights later, at HersheyPark Arena in Hershey, Pennsylvania, Lower Merion met western champion Erie Cathedral Prep for the state Class AAAA title. It was an intense, emotional game between two talented but very different teams. Lower Merion, of course, wanted to run as often as possible. Meanwhile, the Ramblers of Erie Cathedral Prep wanted to do as little rambling as possible. They were a methodical, disciplined team whose only hope of winning was to control the pace of the game.

For a while their strategy worked beautifully. Erie Cathedral Prep, which came in with a 24–6 record, used solid defense and a patient offense to slow the game to a crawl. Kobe, double-teamed whenever he touched the ball, went scoreless in the first quarter, which prompted Cathedral Prep's fans, like Cedar Cliff's, to chant "Overrated! Overrated!" In this game, however, there was a difference. Lower Merion guard Dan Pangrazio, perhaps the team's best outside shooter, was out with a leg injury, which meant the Ramblers could take more risks on the defensive end. They shut out Kobe in the first quarter, and even though he scored eight points in the second quarter, Cathedral Prep still took a 21–15 lead into the locker room at halftime.

As it had so often throughout the season, Lower Merion responded to the pressure. With Kobe and Jermaine Griffin leading the way, the Aces scored the first 11 points of the third quarter to take a 26–21 advantage. As the third quarter came to a close, Lower Merion held what appeared to be a comfortable six-point lead. But the Ramblers were resilient. They fought back, and with 3:30 left in the game John Trocki scored on a layup to put Cathedral Prep ahead, 41–39.

Two free throws by Kobe tied the score at 41–41, and two more by guard Omar Hatcher—filling in for Pangrazio—gave the Aces a 43–41 lead with 2:43 remaining. They never trailed again, although Cathedral Prep had several chances to tie the score. In fact, Lower Merion's fans weren't able to breathe a collective sigh of relief until the final moments. With 30 seconds left and the Aces holding a 45–43 lead, Cathedral Prep's Julian Banks drove the baseline and threw up a difficult running shot. When the ball rolled off the rim, Kobe snared the rebound. He quickly dribbled up the floor and passed ahead to Hatcher, who cruised in for the game-clinching layup.

Moments later the crowd spilled onto the floor as the Lower Merion Aces embraced. One by one the players accepted their gold medals. Then, in a tradition nearly as old as the game of basketball itself, they took turns climbing a ladder and snipped away pieces of the net. They had earned the right to celebrate, to savor the moment. After all, the last time Lower Merion had won a state title, none of these kids was even born. In fact, most of their parents weren't even born.

Still, it wasn't long before reporters surrounded Kobe Bryant and began questioning him about his future plans. *What's it going to be, Kobe—La Salle? Villanova? Duke? Maybe straight to the NBA? Come on, Kobe . . . what's next?*

The best high school player in America looked out over the sea of microphones and cameras and notebooks . . . and smiled.

"I'm going to take a shower," he said. "Then I'm going to get dressed, and I'm going to party."

3

"I'M TAKING MY TALENT TO THE NBA"

Not long after Lower Merion's victory in the Pennsylvania Class AAAA state championship game, the honors began pouring in for Kobe. With 2,883 points in his four-year varsity career, he had become the leading scorer in southeastern Pennsylvania history, surpassing, among others, Hall of Fame center Wilt Chamberlain (2,359). He was named to the *Parade* and McDonald's All-America teams, and was chosen national high school player of the year by numerous publications, including *USA Today*.

For most high school seniors, April signals the end of a career, a time to relax and reflect on the accomplishments of the previous four years. Not for Kobe. For him the springtime months brought more basketball and more publicity, and the intense heat of an all-out recruiting war. Unlike many of the top athletes in his class, Kobe had postponed making any decisions about college until after his final season. So, naturally, the speculation about where he would continue his career reached a fever pitch in the weeks and months following his last game in a Lower Merion uniform.

Kobe was coy. He revealed almost nothing to the reporters who followed his every move, who cornered him after every tournament and all-star game. Instead, he would politely tell them that he had not yet made up his mind. That was the truth, too. He really hadn't decided. On the one hand, he liked the idea of going to college. He was obviously an intelligent kid, as evidenced by his solid B average and 1,080 score on the Scholastic Achievement Test, which made him attractive not only to the best basketball programs in the NCAA, but to some of the top academic schools as well. Kobe knew he'd enjoy the intellectual and athletic challenges that he would encounter at a school like Duke, for example. The Blue Devils played in the ultra-competitive Atlantic Coast Conference and were a perennial Top 20 team. They also had rigorous academic standards. Kobe knew he would fit in well there.

But he also relished the idea of doing something only a handful of basketball players had ever attempted: jumping directly from high school to the NBA. It was almost unheard of for a high school player to sign a professional contract. Rarer still was the athlete who made the transition smoothly. Moses Malone was the first. In 1974, after graduating from high school in

We want to hear your feedback!

Complete our survey at

www.barnesandnoblefeedback.com

or

Text BN to 345345

Your survey code is 9200209-728941

Enter for a chance to win one of twenty
$25 B&N gift cards drawn monthly.

No purchase necessary. Ends 4/30/2019.
Must be legal resident of the 50 US,
including DC and 21+.
Void where prohibited.
Visit www.barnesandnoblefeedback.com for
complete details and official rules.

the date of return, (ii) when a gift certificate is presented within 60 days of purchase, (iii) for textbooks, (iv) when the original tender is PayPal, or (v) for products purchased at Barnes & Noble College bookstores that are listed for sale in the Barnes & Noble Booksellers inventory management system.

Opened music CDs, DVDs, vinyl records, audio books may not be returned, and can be exchanged only for the same title and only if defective. NOOKs purchased from other retailers or sellers are returnable only to the retailer or seller from which they are purchased, pursuant to such retailer's or seller's return policy. Magazines, newspapers, eBooks, digital downloads, and used books are not returnable or exchangeable. Defective NOOKs may be exchanged at the store in accordance with the applicable warranty.

Returns or exchanges will not be permitted (i) after 14 days or without receipt or (ii) for product not carried by Barnes & Noble or Barnes & Noble.com.

Policy on receipt may appear in two sections.

Return Policy

With a sales receipt or Barnes & Noble.com packing slip, a full refund in the original form of payment will be issued from any Barnes & Noble Booksellers store for returns of undamaged NOOKs, new and unread books, and unopened and undamaged music CDs, DVDs, vinyl records, toys/games and audio books made within 14 days of purchase from a Barnes & Noble Booksellers store or Barnes & Noble.com with the below exceptions:

A store credit for the purchase price will be issued (i)

Petersburg, Virginia, he signed with the Utah Stars of the American Basketball Association. When the ABA folded two years later, Malone joined the NBA. A thickly muscled 6–10, 260-pound center, he went on to become one of the greatest players the league has ever known. In a career that spanned two decades he was named most valuable player three times; he also led the Philadelphia 76ers to the NBA championship in 1983.

Darryl Dawkins and Bill Willoughby tried to follow in Malone's footsteps a few years later, but did not have nearly as much success. Shawn Kemp made the jump in 1989 and eventually became one of the NBA's top power forwards. But he was almost 20 years old when he played his first professional game. More inspiring to Kobe was the play of Kevin Garnett, a 6–11 forward from Chicago's Farragut Academy who decided in 1995 to skip college and enter the NBA. The Minnesota Timberwolves made Garnett the fifth pick in the draft, and his rookie year coincided with Kobe's senior year in high school. Garnett quickly became a starter with the Timberwolves and showed glimpses of the all-star he would soon become.

It was only natural for Kobe to look at Garnett and think: *If he can do it, why can't I?*

Of course, there were substantial differences between Kobe Bryant and Kevin Garnett. In fact, there were substantial differences between

Kobe and each of the men who had previously made the gigantic leap from high school to the NBA. First of all, not one of them had demonstrated Kobe's ability in the classroom. He was a superior student as well as a gifted basketball player. Unlike his predecessors, Kobe's options were almost limitless. He had his choice of schools. Second, Kobe was not nearly as physically imposing as the players who had gone before him. They were big men—centers and forwards, each nearly seven feet tall. Kobe was 6–6 and rail-thin. Yes, he was extraordinarily quick, and he could jump out of the gym. He also had a great outside shot. Still, it wasn't unreasonable to think he might have difficulty adjusting to the muscular world of the NBA.

Even Kobe, who never lacked confidence, understood that if he decided to bypass college, he'd be taking a tremendous risk. "I'm a little fella," he said. "I know it will be a big adjustment if I try to make the jump. It's a lot of hard work."

Speculation followed Kobe wherever he went in the spring of 1996, including Pittsburgh, site of the McDonald's All-American game, one of the premier all-star events in high school basketball. Kobe was the most famous and talented player at the Civic Arena on March 31, just as his father had been twenty-four years earlier. Joe Bryant had played in this same building in the Dapper Dan Classic as a senior at Bartram High School in 1972. In fact, Joe had been named MVP of that game, which featured Pennsylvania's best scholastic players competing against an all-star team from the rest of the country.

Sitting in the stands, watching his son race up and down the very same court, Joe Bryant could only marvel at the passage of time. "I feel so old," he told the *Philadelphia Inquirer.* "That other game was so, so long ago."

The son did not quite match his father's performance. Although Kobe scored 13 points in just 19 minutes of playing time, MVP honors went to Shaheen Holloway of Elizabeth, New Jersey. The McDonald's event also featured a slam dunk contest. Kobe managed only a third-place finish, but his overall performance still had the crowd—which included scouts from dozens of colleges and more than twenty NBA teams—salivating.

And wondering . . .

What will Kobe do next?

"I think Kobe is, in my mind, the best player I've seen in this class," Bob Gibbons, a national recruiting analyst, told the *Charlotte Observer.* "He's advanced in the fundamentals and his knowledge of the game. His performance in the McDonald's game wasn't significant, but Kobe . . . he ranks among the top prospects I've seen in twenty years.

"Is he physically ready for the NBA? No. Is he mentally ready for the NBA? Probably not. But his experience playing against the 76ers, and his dad having spent time in the league . . . I would be surprised if he doesn't go pro. It's a risky proposition, but it's hard to tell a seventeen-year-old he can't do it."

Among the NBA representatives in the crowd was Bob Bass, director of basketball operations for the Charlotte Hornets. Eventually it would be the Hornets who would take a chance on Kobe in the draft, so obviously the team was impressed with his ability. But on this day Bass chose his words carefully. "If he were to come out, somebody would draft him," Bass told the *Charlotte Observer*. "But how long would it be before he could help a team? Kevin Garnett might be an exception in that he played well this season—at least since mid-season. But 82 games, 100 practices . . . you immediately think they can't do it. I'd hate to have to draft a high school player because you have to wait for them to develop."

Bass' point was hard to dispute. Any player who attenpts to go directly from high school to the NBA faces enormous hurdles. In all likelihood, it will take him years to clear those barriers. In addition to being at a physical disadvantage, he also lacks the experience that he would have acquired in college. If Kobe chose to take the college route, he surely would be an immediate starter. He would get 30 to 35 minutes a night. His game would develop naturally. Under the right coach, he'd learn more about the fundamentals of basketball. Unlike high school, he'd be surrounded by players who would challenge and complement him. Two, three, or four years down the road, he'd move smoothly to the next level: the NBA.

As an eighteen-year-old professional, though, he'd be learning on the job. And if his playing time was limited, the educational process could be slow and painful. This was the dilemma facing Kobe Bryant.

Two weeks later, at the Roundball Classic in Detroit, more than 13,000 fans showed up at the Palace for another all-star game featuring twenty of the best high school basketball players in the nation. As he had been in Pittsburgh, Kobe was the center of attention, even though several of the young men involved had yet to select a college. At a press conference the day before the game, Kobe was pressed by members of the media to give them some clue as to what his decision would be. By now, Kobe was accustomed to this routine. He simply smiled and gave the usual diplomatic response: "I'm going to take my time and talk to my family before I make a decision."

Kobe's performance in the Roundball Classic was electrifying. He scored 21 points, including two on a rim-rattling dunk over 6–10

Jamaal Magliore (who would go on to help Kentucky win the 1998 NCAA championship), and two more on an acrobatic shot in the lane with his back to the basket. Kobe's East All-Stars lost to the West, 127–117, and Tim Thomas, another future NBA player, was named MVP of the East. But it was Kobe who put on the best show. And it was Kobe who naturally drew the biggest media crowd after the game. Unfortunately, he had nothing new to reveal. There would be many more heart-to-heart discussions with his father, he said. He even planned to seek out Kevin Garnett and ask about life as a professional athlete. It was only April, Kobe figured, and this was the most important decision of his life. There was no reason to hurry.

"I'm going to listen to everyone's advice," he told the *Detroit News*. "It all depends if I'm ready mentally and physically for the NBA."

On the afternoon of April 29, 1996, as another school day came to an end, students and teachers at Lower Merion High School began filing into the gymnasium. A special assembly had been called, and everyone knew the reason why: Kobe Bryant had made a decision. Finally, after months of anticipation, he was going to announce his future plans.

But what did that mean? Speculation and rumors were rampant, but outside of his family and a few close friends, no one knew for sure what Kobe was going to say when he strolled up to the microphone that day. In Philadelphia, naturally, there was still some hope that Kobe would follow his dad to La Salle. Joe Bryant had been a star there two decades earlier, and his status as an assistant coach certainly kept the Explorers in the running. La Salle's basketball program was not nearly as high-powered as the others that were engaged in the recruiting war for Kobe's services, but he had a strong emotional bond with the school. For years he had been attending La Salle's games and practices, and using the school's training facilities. It had become like a second home.

By the spring of Kobe's senior year it was apparent that he had narrowed his choices to three: La Salle, Duke, or the NBA. Philadelphia basketball fans understandably hoped he would decide to stay home and help the Explorers recapture some of their past glory. They envisioned Kobe following the career path taken by Tom Gola more than forty years earlier. Gola was a local star who went on to lead La Salle to the 1954 NCAA championship. He played professionally for the 76ers and later became a city councilman in Philadelphia. Gola managed to carve out a wonderful career and life for himself without ever straying far from his Philadelphia roots. Was it so ridiculous to think that Kobe might do the same thing?

Well, yes.

"It just wasn't going to happen," La Salle coach Phil Martelli would later tell the *Orange County Register*. "He was just beyond that stage. Kobe is a genius. He's like one of those kids who graduates from college at the age of thirteen.

"The great thing is what a good kid he is. He comes here in our gym in the summer and plays against the pros. And then he does the weights and shoots by himself at night. I tell our players, 'Check out his work ethic.' But what I remember most is, every day he came by, he'd make a point to stop by the office and say thanks for letting him use the gym. *Letting him use the gym!* Now, that's class."

Gregg Downer, too, felt it would be a mistake for Kobe to accept a scholarship from La Salle. He would have enjoyed having the opportunity to watch Kobe develop in the collegiate ranks, and he knew it would have been a wonderful thing for Philadelphia. But Downer, like Martelli, knew that it probably wasn't the best thing for Kobe.

"We have a pretty close relationship, and it wasn't unusual for us to go behind closed doors and talk one-on-one about a lot of things," Downer said. "I think his family, especially his father, was really in the best position to talk to him about his decision, but I did give him my opinion in a conversation we had about a week before he made his announcement. My opinion was that if Kobe was going to go to college, I was hoping it would be Duke. I thought that was the best place for him—socially, athletically, academically."

Kobe thought so, too. In his heart, though, he knew that what he really wanted was an opportunity to play in the NBA. Not in three or four years, but right away, while there was still an opportunity to compete against some of the players he had idolized as a kid, players he considered to be the best.

"As a coach I always encouraged Kobe to follow his dreams," Downer said. "I encourage all of my players to shoot for the stars, and it was very evident that his dream was to play in the NBA, to get on the floor against Michael Jordan and Charles Barkley. And the time to do that was kind of dwindling."

Just as basketball games at Lower Merion High School had been transformed into spectacles during Kobe's last two years, the press conference to announce his decision was anything but an ordinary affair. In addition to representatives from various local media outlets, there were cameras from ESPN and reporters from such prestigious publications as the *Washington Post* and *New York Times*. Standing in the back of the gym were members of the popular singing group Boyz II Men, who called Philadelphia home and Kobe Bryant a friend. Clearly, this was not just a high school kid making a decision about where he would play basketball next.

This was a young man on the verge of super-stardom.

As Kobe slowly approached the podium, a buzz swept through the gymnasium. He wore a crisp new suit for the occasion; sunglasses were perched neatly atop his shaved head. There was a look of nervousness on his face, or maybe it was just excitement.

As Kobe leaned into the microphone, the gym fell silent. "Hi, I'm Kobe Bryant," he said, as if anyone didn't already know that, "and I've decided to take my talent to, uhh . . ." Kobe paused and smiled. He stroked his chin theatrically, as if he wanted to give the impression that he hadn't quite made up his mind yet. But he had, of course. He was simply teasing everyone. He was enjoying this moment in the spotlight, soaking it all in.

After a few seconds Kobe went on. "Well, I've decided to skip college and take my talent to the NBA." One newspaper writer later wondered, in print, if Kobe would be accompanying his talent. In the Lower Merion gym, though, there was no such sarcasm to be found. The entire room burst into wild applause. Squeals of approval echoed off the walls. If anyone here was disappointed by the decision, they sure did a good job of hiding their displeasure. Kobe, meanwhile, seemed like the happiest kid on the planet. He shook hands, signed autographs, and gracefully fielded questions from the media. He didn't predict greatness, or even instant success. Instead, he played the role of a diplomat. Kobe wanted everyone to know that a lot of thought had gone into this decision. He was fully aware of the challenges that lay ahead. At the same time he made it quite clear that confidence wouldn't be an issue.

"I know I'll have to work extra hard, and I know this is a big step," he said. "But I can do it. It's the opportunity of a lifetime. It's time to seize it while I'm young. I don't know if I can reach the stars or the moon. If I fall off the cliff, so be it."

Predictably, the backlash against Kobe began almost immediately after he announced his intention to jump directly to the NBA. In a story that appeared in *Sports Illustrated*, Jon Jennings, director of basketball development for the Boston Celtics, was quoted as saying, "I think it's a total mistake. Kevin Garnett was the best high school player I ever saw, and I wouldn't have advised him to jump to the NBA. And Kobe is no Kevin Garnett."

Columnist Mike DeCourcy, writing in the *Sporting News*, attacked on a more personal level, saying, "Questions about the relative fitness of young Kobe Bryant for life in the NBA should have been answered the moment he appeared for the news conference in which he dismissed college basketball as unworthy of even a moment of his time. The shades, man. Way too cool for college."

DeCourcy went on to point out that, financially speaking, Kobe was probably making the right decision. But, he added, "I'm not sure why anyone cares whether he's ready for such a life, because his folks apparently didn't."

That hurt the most. The Bryants were willing to accept criticism of Kobe's athletic ability, but they were understandably stung by comments about their parenting skills. They wanted nothing but the best for their children, and if Kobe really wanted to play in the NBA, then they would stand behind him. Pam Bryant told the *Sporting News*, "Whether it was college or going to the NBA, we're always going to support him. That's what we always do.

"No matter what, my family comes first. I don't care what this one or that one thinks. People can feel or say what they want, but the last time I checked, where I live there are five members in my family. They come first. That's what all of this is about."

It seemed ridiculous for anyone to suggest that Joe Bryant had somehow manipulated his son. Joe and Pam took great pride in knowing that they had raised three thoughtful, intelligent, independent children. When Kobe wanted guidance or advice, Joe was there to dispense it. After all, he had been down this road. He had been a heavily recruited high school athlete, and he had played in the NBA. He had contacts. He could tell Kobe what to expect.

But Joe never pressured his son, never twisted his arm. And he certainly wasn't trying to live through Kobe. The truth, Joe said, was that he liked the idea of Kobe attending a prestigious academic institution. But it was Kobe's decision to make. It was, after all, his life. Joe merely armed his son with as much information as he could provide, and then stepped out of the way.

"I've been fortunate in the sense that I've been around and know the water he's about to tread," Joe told the *Sporting News*. "I don't think you can fault me for having an understanding of what's going on. I've talked to a lot of people, and I've touched a lot of bases. I think Kobe is lucky to have someone who's been there.

"Hey, I would have liked to have seen Kobe go to school for four years and go to Harvard. But is that reality? Would he have stayed in school for one or two years? This was Kobe's dream, so it's his decision."

The Bryants were under siege for weeks. Columnists took shots on a daily basis. Radio talk shows found an endless supply of callers who had an opinion about Kobe's decision. To Gregg Downer, it all seemed ludicrous.

"I didn't like the backlash at all," he said.

"Our radio shows were just on fire with every-body tossing in their two cents' worth. And these were people who really didn't know what they were talking about. There weren't many people fortunate enough to be on the inside, to meet Kobe's family, and to see exactly how good a player he really was. Seeing this kid every day, I knew that he was special. Some of the dunks that he would throw down in practice . . . I would turn to my assistant coaches and say, 'What in the world is the difference between what we just saw and Penny Hardaway or Grant Hill? Is there any possible way he can jump higher? Is there any possible way he can have a longer wingspan?' I was a little unsure about what the difference was. And now, looking back, I realize there was no difference."

Actually, it was hard to see how anyone could fault Kobe for being so ambitious. After all, what was the worst thing that could happen? He would sign a contract for several million dollars and give pro basketball his best effort. If things didn't work out, he could always go to college in two or three years. Unlike most students, he wouldn't have any trouble paying for his tuition. For some reason, though, many observers insisted on criticizing Kobe and his family. Carl Chancellor, writing in the *Akron Beacon Journal*, suggested a possible motive for their anger:

"Let's be real. Those bemoaning Bryant's

decision couldn't care less about the seventeen-year-old's future. What these hypocrites are giving vent to is their jealousy. They are jealous that a kid right out of high school soon will be earning millions of dollars to play basketball. Hey, admit it: I'm jealous of Bryant, too. Wouldn't we all like to be given the opportunity to fulfill a lifelong dream and be paid handsomely to boot? Bryant is one in a million, and probably more like one in 100 million. Telling him he shouldn't enter the NBA is like telling the guy working behind the counter at Dairy Mart not to redeem his winning lottery ticket. The reality is that many high school graduates choose not to go to college. Bryant's career choice just happens to be basketball. Those who do go to college do so with the aim of acquiring the skills they need to become doctors, lawyers, teachers, etc. Obviously, those who know have determined that Bryant already has the skills for the NBA."

True enough. It wasn't as though Kobe was proceeding blindly. His father had many contacts in the world of basketball and had determined that Kobe would surely be a first-round draft pick; in all likelihood, he'd be one of the top fifteen players taken. Yes, there were many stories of players who had left college early in the hope of playing in the NBA, only to discover that they were drafted very late or weren't drafted at all. For those players, sacrificing a college scholarship was a huge mistake. But Joe Bryant had done his homework. He knew that many teams were seriously interested in drafting his son. It was still somewhat of a gamble, but the odds were certainly in Kobe's favor.

Less predictable was Kobe's ability to handle life as a professional athlete. He'd be an eighteen-year-old kid, just a few months out of high school, trying to adjust to a very grown-up world. He'd have lots of money and plenty of time to spend it. He'd be on the road a lot, surrounded by people who wanted to take advantage of him, who wanted to get close to him simply because he was rich and famous. Many young athletes have wasted their talent and destroyed their careers because they spent too much time playing and not enough time working. Some have turned to alcohol or drugs to cope with the pressure.

None of this was news to Kobe. Having grown up in a basketball family, he knew all about life in the NBA. He knew about the temptations and the risks.

"That's perfect," Joe Bryant said in an interview with ESPN Radio a few days after Kobe's announcement. "He's been there. He's seen it. You know the commercial: *Been there, done that*. That's why we feel comfortable with it. We gave him the foundation of life that any family would love to give its children. Kobe is aware of the physical play. There's no doubt about his skills; his skills are there to play. He has to get bigger and stronger, but as I said to one reporter, 'Hey, all these guys are going to be going out to the clubs [after games]. Kobe will be back at the hotel reading a book or playing Nintendo.'"

Indeed, Kobe seemed wise beyond his years. He exhibited a maturity rarely seen in young men drafted after four years of *college*, let alone high school. "He has an inner strength," Kobe's grandmother, Mildred Cox, told the *Philadelphia Inquirer*. "He doesn't need a lot of folks around him, but his real friends, his family, he's true to them. And the rest of the world, the outside things that are going on, he seems to just tune it all out."

Maybe. Then again, there was no question that a part of Kobe relished the spotlight. That much would soon become obvious.

Less than two weeks after announcing his intention to play professionally, Kobe signed a lucrative endorsement contract with Adidas (published reports estimated the deal to be worth approximately $10 million), which immediately announced plans to market a new Kobe Bryant shoe. Some basketball insiders were surprised that Kobe chose Adidas rather than Nike, the industry leader and the employer of many of the NBA's top stars, most notably Michael Jordan. But Kobe wanted to do something different. As he later explained, "Adidas is up-and-coming, on the rise. I wanted to be a part of that. It's easy to just go with the brand that's already at the top, join in and blend in, but that's something I didn't want to do."

Shortly after agreeing on a deal with Adidas, Kobe also signed a contract with the powerful William Morris Agency, which represents many of the biggest stars in the entertainment industry. Never before had William Morris signed a basketball player. In more ways than one, Kobe had become a trail blazer. There was no turning back.

Not that he really wanted to. Kobe seemed to be quite comfortable with his new celebrity. In late May, at the Lower Merion senior prom, he was half of what had to be the youngest and cutest power couple in America. Kobe's date for the evening? None other than Brandy, the teen pop singer and star of the hit television sitcom *Moesha*, who had recently been named one of the "fifty most beautiful people" by *People* magazine.

Kobe and Brandy, who had met at an all-star basketball game in Philadelphia, turned an ordinary high school prom into a media circus. Parents hoping to take snapshots of their elegantly dressed children had to fight for position with photographers and cameramen from an assortment of magazines and tabloid news shows. The glamour couple showed up fashionably late. They signed autographs, had dinner, danced for a while, and tried to act like normal seventeen-year-old kids at a senior prom. Of course, that really wasn't possible. As Brandy already knew, and as Kobe was quickly discovering, fame changes everything.

4

DRAFT DODGING

Kobe spent a lot of time on the road in the weeks leading up to the 1996 NBA draft. But he didn't have much time for sightseeing or relaxing. He was working.

The draft is perhaps the most important event on the NBA calendar. There are two rounds. Each of the league's 29 teams selects one player in each round. That means only 58 players will be drafted. A lot is at stake in the draft. Careers are built. Fortunes are won and lost. The foundations for championships are poured.

If a team makes a mistake and chooses a player who turns out to be less than advertised, it can cost the franchise millions of dollars. A series of bad draft picks will result in a team floundering near the bottom of the NBA standings year after year. When a team loses more often than it wins, fans get angry. When fans get angry, they stop coming to games. And when arenas have a lot of empty seats, people tend to lose their jobs. So, naturally, everyone is more than a little nervous on draft day.

There is no way to eliminate the element of risk from the draft process. No matter how successful a player is in college (or in foreign leagues, which have produced a number of NBA players in recent years), there is no guarantee that he will make it in the NBA. Just about every team has felt the sting of a botched draft pick. Occasionally, players taken early in the first round not only fail to meet expectations, but barely contribute at all. For whatever reason they are unable to adapt to life in the NBA. Perhaps they've already reached a physical peak. Or maybe they weren't really all that good in the first place. Some players lack the mental toughness to compete against the best athletes in the world on a nightly basis. Others lose their ambition as soon as they sign their first million-dollar contract. The hunger that has carried them to the NBA suddenly disappears.

Conversely, some players develop beyond anyone's expectations. Michael Jordan is considered perhaps the greatest player in the history of the NBA. But when he left the University of North Carolina in 1984, he wasn't even considered the best player in his own class. Jordan, in fact, was the third—not first—player chosen in that year's draft.

The people who decide which players will be selected—coaches, scouts, owners, general managers—really don't like to gamble. So, to improve the odds of making the right choices, they do a lot of homework before the draft. They conduct lengthy interviews in an effort to determine if the player seems emotionally prepared for the NBA. They hold rigorous workouts. And they watch hours and hours of videotape. They study every aspect of the player's game, dissecting his strengths and weaknesses.

Can he shoot? Can he dribble? Can he play defense? Is he a good jumper? How well does he see the floor? Does he like to pass, or is he selfish?

If you watch enough game tape, most of these questions will be answered. In the case of Kobe Bryant, however, there was a bit of a problem. While every Division I college basketball team routinely tapes its games, most high schools do not. The few tapes that were available provided little insight, since Kobe was always the most talented player on the floor in high school. It was hard to fault prospective employers for wanting a bit more information. They saw Kobe dunking over dozens of slower, smaller teenagers, and they wondered if he could do the same against grown men.

As a result, in the months of May and June, Kobe spent more time than most draftees working out for NBA teams. He traveled from city to city, meeting with coaches and front office personnel from just about every NBA franchise. "It's all pretty much the same," he said of the experience. "Shoot some jump shots, dribble the ball."

Kobe impressed just about everyone with his talent and maturity. In most interviews he was questioned about his heart and desire, and about the difficulty of trying to compete with grown men when you're only eighteen years old. By this time Kobe had grown accustomed to hearing skeptical comments. His confidence, though, was never shaken. When anyone suggested that he was making a mistake by not sharpening his game in college before turning pro, Kobe quietly but proudly stood up for himself.

"I accept that as a challenge," he told the Associated Press. "I'm going to go out there and work twice as hard to prove them wrong. When I first came back from Italy, I had a lot of people saying I couldn't start on my high school basketball team as a freshman at fourteen. People were saying I'd never be able to win a state championship, that I couldn't do this, I couldn't do that. Once I was in my senior year, I really had proven everything I had to prove. Then I won the state championship, and that was icing on the cake. Now I'm starting over again, and that feels good.

"I'm not afraid to fail," Kobe added. "When I'm forty, if I sit back and I say, 'Man, I went to the NBA, I gave it my all, and I failed,' it happens. But I couldn't accept not going to the NBA and giving my all. I can't accept that."

News travels swiftly along the NBA grapevine, so it wasn't long before the word leaked out: Kobe's workouts were sensational! As a result his stock began to rise. Even teams that weren't in a position to draft Kobe wanted to take a look. The Philadelphia 76ers, for example, had the very first pick in the draft and were expected to take Georgetown University's sensational point guard Allen Iverson. But Kobe was a hometown kid with a lot of hometown fans, and the 76ers wanted to make sure they weren't missing anything.

"Our basketball staff sees how good a prospect we think he is," 76ers general manager Brad Greenberg said after watching Kobe work out just a week before the draft. "He's a very young guy, and he's going to develop an awful lot over the next couple of years. The only way to see if that's going to happen is to spend some time with him."

The Los Angeles Lakers were another team that became deeply interested in Kobe after meeting with him and watching him work out. "It was an absolutely incredible workout," said Jerry West, the Lakers' executive vice president of basketball operations. "He's a potential NBA all-star." The Lakers would have to do some wheeling and dealing if they had any hope of getting Kobe. They had the twenty-seventh pick in the draft, and Kobe would certainly be gone by then. This fact was not lost on West, a Hall of Fame guard who once starred for the Lakers and who is now considered one of the best evaluators of talent in the NBA. In an interview with the *Los Angeles Times,* Arn Tellem, Kobe's agent, recalled a conversation with West shortly after Kobe's audition for the Lakers: "After the workout—I'll never forget it—when Jerry called up, he said it was the best workout he'd ever seen in his life. At the end of the conversation he said, 'We've got to figure out a way to get him here.'"

Few people outside the Lakers organization were aware of it at the time, but already the wheels were in motion. Kobe Bryant was on his way to becoming a Los Angeles Laker.

On June 26, 1996, the NBA draft was broadcast live to a national television audience from the Meadowlands in East Rutherford, New Jersey. The draft is always a tense affair, especially for the players involved, because they are never quite sure which team will draft them, or how long they'll have to wait before their name is called. Teams often try to strengthen themselves through last-minute trades, which can make matters even more confusing and dramatic. When the magic moment finally arrives, the player is summoned to a podium and handed a jersey and baseball cap from his new team.

This particular draft began predictably enough, but soon became filled with intrigue. NBA commissioner David Stern strolled up to the microphone early in the evening and announced that the Philadelphia 76ers had selected Allen Iverson, just as everyone suspected they would. The second choice was Marcus Camby, a 6–11 center from the University of Massachusetts who was the consensus college player of the year; he was taken by the Toronto Raptors, just as Toronto general manager Isiah Thomas had promised. The third pick belonged to the Vancouver Grizzlies, who chose Shareef Abdur-Rahim, a 6–10 forward from the University of California-Berkeley.

Then came the surprises. The Milwaukee Bucks took point guard Stephon Marbury of Georgia Tech with the fourth pick, and the Minnesota Timberwolves chose Connecticut guard Ray Allen with the fifth. Within minutes the two players were summoned back on stage as Stern announced that the Bucks had traded Marbury to the Timberwolves in exchange for Allen and a number one draft choice in either 1999 or 2000. The two young men swapped caps, shook hands, and smiled.

"I can't believe it," Marbury said. "It happened so quick. I was with Milwaukee for like a minute."

The 1996 draft was the youngest in NBA history. Marbury, who left Georgia Tech after his freshman year, was one of five teenagers taken in the top fourteen. Only two college seniors were included in that group, and one player was a *high school* senior. His name, of course, was Kobe Bryant.

The Charlotte Hornets drafted Kobe with the thirteenth pick. The selection surprised many observers, including Kobe, since Charlotte was one of the few teams for whom he had not worked out. Still, he seemed thrilled to have been drafted at all. "I was sitting back there watching the television like everyone else, and I saw the cameras moving toward my table," Kobe said. "I was starting to get a little nervous about what was going on. Then they said, 'Kobe Bryant.' That's when it kind of hit me: I'm an NBA player! Now it's time to go in there and try to do some work."

As usual, Kobe was accompanied by his entire family, which made the moment even more emotional. "It was pretty difficult because I had my mother there squeezing my thigh and my sister there squeezing my hands and my father there winking at me all teary-eyed," he said.

When Kobe took his place on stage, he was handed a Hornets baseball cap. The cap's colors, purple and teal, matched Kobe's necktie. A coincidence . . . or fate? Kobe didn't know. But he sounded happy to be going to Charlotte, where one of his teammates would be Larry Johnson. Johnson was famous not only for his basketball ability, but for a sneaker commercial in which he portrayed a hoop-playing version of his own grandmother—a high-flying, trash-talking, rimrattlin', hip-hoppin' senior citizen. "I get to go out there and mess it up with Grandmama!" Kobe said.

Not necessarily. Within an hour trade rumors were swirling about the Meadowlands. When Charlotte coach Dave Cowens told reporters that he felt Kobe was just "a kid" who would probably have a difficult time fitting in with the Hornets, it became clear that this was not a marriage made in heaven. Apparently, Charlotte had drafted Kobe with the intention of trading him—as soon as possible. Although they thought Kobe had tremendous potential, what they really wanted was an established big man, either a center or a forward who had proven ability; owning the rights to a potential superstar like Kobe Bryant could help them obtain such a player.

A lot of teams were interested in bidding for Kobe's services, including the Los Angeles Lakers. They had taken point guard Derek Fisher of Arkansas-Little Rock with the twenty-fourth pick in the draft. But their sights were still set on Kobe Bryant. Before the draft even ended, Jerry West was on the phone with Charlotte's front office. "They've said Kobe is available, and we're certainly interested," West said that evening. "They said they drafted him to move him. If so, they'll have a lot of teams talking to them. This guy is not a typical seventeen-year-old kid. He doesn't play like a seventeen-year-old."

For the next few days West and the Lakers aggressively pursued a deal that would bring Kobe to Los Angeles. Some newspaper columnists criticized Kobe for what they perceived to be arrogance. They thought he was trying to orchestrate a trade, and that he was insisting on playing only in Los Angeles. According to Kobe's agent, however, that wasn't true. Yes, Kobe liked the idea of working and living in Los Angeles because of its tremendous marketing potential and gentle climate—and because the Lakers were a young team on the rise. But he would have been happy playing in Charlotte, too.

"People need to make themselves aware of the situation," Arn Tellem told the *Philadelphia Inquirer.* "Then their opinions might change a bit. I learned about the possibility, just the possibility, of him going to Los Angeles the day of the draft. Once I knew that, we wanted to make it happen. He had nothing against Charlotte. It's just that once we knew L.A. was a possibility, we did everything we could to make that happen. You have to remember something: the Hornets drafted him to trade him, not to keep him. It wasn't that Kobe didn't want to be there. Kobe knew that they didn't want him."

That was the truth. The Hornets *didn't* want Kobe. They wanted Vlade Divac, the Lakers' 7-foot–1, 255-pound center. Divac, at twenty-eight years of age, was a proven front-court player. He had averaged nearly 13 points a game in seven

NBA seasons, and had been the Lakers' leading rebounder for four consecutive seasons.

Parting with Divac would not be easy for the Lakers. He had led Yugoslavia to a silver medal in the 1988 Summer Olympics. A year later he came to Los Angeles and became one of the top rookies in the NBA. He had been a vital and popular member of the team ever since. If the Lakers wanted Kobe, however, they would have to make sacrifices, and Divac was part of the bargain.

There was another piece to the puzzle. The hottest free agent in the NBA in the summer of 1996 was all-star center Shaquille O'Neal, whose contract with the Orlando Magic had expired. The Lakers were pursuing O'Neal as vigorously as they were pursuing Kobe, but they had to figure out a way to make the deal work financially. The NBA's salary cap places strict limits on how much a team is allowed to spend on its players. If they wanted to sign Shaq, the Lakers would first have to reduce the size of their payroll. So trading Divac, one of the team's highest-paid players, would solve two problems: it would leave the Lakers with enough money to sign Shaq, and it would bring Kobe to Los Angeles.

If everything went according to Jerry West's plans, two of the most exciting young players in the game would soon be wearing the purple and gold of the Los Angeles Lakers.

5

I LOVE L.A.!

As Kobe Bryant strolled through Los Angeles International Airport on the morning of July 11, 1996, he was approached by a stranger. The man had taken one look at Kobe's size and athletic build and figured he must be a basketball player. But he couldn't quite place the face. So he asked Kobe where he played ball.

"I started to say Lower Merion High School," Kobe later recalled. "And then I stopped and thought for a second, and said, 'I guess I'm a Laker.' That brought a real big smile to my face."

And well it should have. Kobe had indeed just been traded to the Lakers for Vlade Divac. The first phase of Jerry West's master plan was complete. Within a week Shaquille O'Neal would leave Orlando and join Kobe in Los Angeles, and suddenly the Lakers would look like a team with enough talent to win a championship—if not in the upcoming season, then certainly in the near future. Not only did they have Kobe and Shaq, but they also had a brilliant young point guard named Nick Van Exel, a versatile center/forward named Elden Campbell, and a smooth-shooting swing man named Eddie Jones. Who could blame Lakers fans for thinking that this group of athletes were capable of restoring the franchise to its former glory?

The Lakers, you see, are one of the most successful franchises in NBA history. Long before they came to Los Angeles, they were winning championships. The first came in 1948, when an agile giant named George Mikan, the game's first great big man, led the Minneapolis Lakers to the National Basketball League title. The following year the Lakers won the Basketball Association of America championship, and in 1950 they joined the NBA and immediately became the best team in that league as well. In fact, Minneapolis won four NBA titles in the 1950s, establishing a tradition of excellence that continues today.

In 1960 the franchise was uprooted and moved west. There aren't a lot of lakes in Southern California; nevertheless, the nickname traveled with the team, and the Los Angeles Lakers were born. The Lakers were one of the NBA's most consistent and successful franchises in the 1960s and early 1970s. With sharpshooters Jerry West and Gail Goodrich in the back court, Hall of Famer Elgin Baylor in the front court, and Wilt Chamberlain in the pivot, the Lakers were a tremendously potent offensive team. They won six Western Division titles in the 1960s, an incredible feat. Unfortunately for Los Angeles, there happened to be another great team in the NBA at that time: the Boston Celtics. Five times the Lakers lost to the Celtics in the NBA finals. The sixth time, after the 1969–70 season, they were beaten by the New York Knicks.

The 1970s began much as the 1960s had ended, with the Lakers winning a divisional championship in 1970–71 and then losing in the NBA finals. This time the opponent was the Milwaukee Bucks, who were led by 7-foot–2 center Kareem Abdul-Jabbar. In the spring of 1972, the heartache finally ended. The Lakers were arguably the best team in NBA history that year. They won 33 consecutive games (the longest winning streak in professional sports history) and captured the Pacific Division title by a margin of 18 games! Jerry West led the NBA in assists, and Gail Goodrich averaged a team-high 25.9 points as the Lakers established an NBA record with 69 victories (a mark that stood until 1995–96, when it was broken by Michael Jordan and the Chicago Bulls). In the NBA finals, the Lakers routed the Knicks, four games to one.

By the start of the 1975–76 season, Chamberlain had been replaced at center by Abdul-Jabbar, who was obtained in a trade with the Bucks. At the time it seemed like a risky move—the Lakers gave up four players in order to acquire Abdul-Jabbar—but eventually the trade would be viewed as one of the best bargains in NBA history. Abdul-Jabbar spent 14 seasons in Los Angeles. By the time he retired, he had led the Lakers to five NBA championships and was the league's all-time scoring leader.

But even Kareem couldn't carry a team by himself. It wasn't until Ervin "Magic" Johnson came along in 1979 that the Lakers once again became champions. Magic, a sensational 6-foot–9 point guard out of Michigan State University, brought both style and substance to the Great Western Forum, where the Lakers played their home games. With extraordinary ball-handling skills, an uncanny ability to see every inch of the floor, and boundless enthusiasm, Magic quickly became the team's leader. His versatility was most evident in Game 6 of the 1980 NBA finals. When Abdul-Jabbar was forced out of the game with an injury and the Lakers needed a center, they turned to Magic, despite the fact that he was only a rookie and hadn't played the position since high school. Magic responded brilliantly. He had 42 points and 15 rebounds as the Lakers defeated the Philadelphia 76ers to clinch their first NBA title in eight years.

Two years later, assistant coach Pat Riley became the Lakers' new head coach. His promotion signaled the beginning of a long and entertaining era at the Forum known as ... *Showtime!* The Lakers of the 1980s were an immensely talented team. They were also a lot of fun to watch. Magic ran the fast break like no one before him, often finishing with a perfect no-look pass to James Worthy, a 6–9 forward out of North Carolina. Byron Scott nailed three-pointers. Michael Cooper was the defensive ace. Kareem was the master of the sky hook, a beautiful one-handed shot that was virtually unstoppable.

And Riley was the master of motivation, the man who brought all of these elements together. He was a deeply competitive and philosophical coach who knew precisely what to say in order to get the most out of each player. Riley led the Lakers to the NBA championship in 1981–82, in his first season as a head coach. He won a second title in 1984–85, and a third in 1986–87. The players had barely finished celebrating that title when Riley guaranteed that his team would repeat as champions. And they did. The Lakers won 62 regular-season games in 1987–88 and became the first team since the great Boston Celtics teams of the 1960s to win back-to-back NBA titles. They defeated the Detroit Pistons, four games to three, in the finals.

This legacy of greatness was hardly news to Kobe Bryant. Although he had grown up in Italy and played high school ball in Philadelphia, and despite the fact that his father had been a member of the 76ers, Kobe was a big fan of the Los Angeles Lakers. Unlike many of his contemporaries, Kobe was a student of the game of basketball. He had a sense of history. He knew all about the players who had come before him, players who had made the NBA such a success. Kobe had confidence in himself, but he also had respect for the men who had made it possible for him to become a millionaire at the age of seventeen.

To Byron Scott, who played part of the 1996–97 season with Kobe, the young superstar's attitude was refreshing. "He's different," Scott told the *Los Angeles Times*. "He would have done well in the eighties with us. At least, he showed me a tremendous amount of respect, back when we were working at practice and I would tell him things that we would try to work on, and I don't think he was doing it for show. He was very interested in hearing about our team in the eighties, and we would sit down and talk about that. He is totally different than a lot of guys that are coming into the league, with the big heads and the egos and things like that."

If Kobe was happy on draft day, he was positively euphoric on July 12, when he was formally introduced to the Los Angeles media during a press conference at the Forum. Although he seemed remarkably poised for one so young, he could not hide his enthusiasm over the prospect of playing in Los Angeles. "I'm very excited to be here," he said. "It's a dream come true to play in the NBA and to come to a team like L.A. that has a great history, great players like Magic Johnson and Kareem Abdul-Jabbar. It was a team I looked up to when I was growing up, and now here I am playing pickup basketball with Magic Johnson at UCLA."

The Lakers were equally excited about the newest member of their team. Jerry West is not prone to overstatement. He chooses his words carefully, like any smart businessman. But when it came to Kobe Bryant, he could barely contain himself.

"We think this young man is one of the most exciting young prospects we've seen in a long time," West said. "People asked me a lot of questions before the draft—would we draft a high school player? My response was always that we would try to get the best basketball player we could to help our team become a better team."

Kobe, obviously, was that player. In time, West promised, he would be one of the most accomplished athletes in the NBA. "We think this racehorse is going to be an incredible player," he gushed. "In five or six years the people of Los Angeles will be talking about him in very high terms. It's not a necessity he plays a lot of minutes for us right away. Obviously our coaching staff will have a chance to work with him and further his development. We know there will be some growing pains in the process, but we are prepared to accept this challenge. I think that Kobe is more than prepared to accept his part of the challenge."

Lakers coach Del Harris was equally impressed with Kobe. He was, however, reluctant to slap a label on any of his players, Kobe included. So, when reporters pressed Harris for an assessment of Kobe's talents, the coach was somewhat evasive.

"If you want to know what his game is like now, it's a bit like Eddie Jones, who plays one, two, or three," Harris said. "Our type of game is very free-flowing, and Kobe has an all-around game that will thrive in our system. I don't think it serves Kobe well to put a label on him. There's nothing about him that hasn't impressed me. If you want me to start talking about him, we're talking about Clark Kent here."

Which also meant they were talking about Superman. This wasn't exactly news to Eddie Jones, who had known Kobe for several years. The two had, in fact, become close friends during Jones' time at Temple University in Philadelphia. They hung out together and frequently played one-on-one. Kobe was thrilled that he would now be Jones' teammate, and not simply because they'd be playing basketball together. At twenty-three years of age, Jones was like a big brother to Kobe. He wouldn't lecture Kobe, but he would offer advice. And Kobe was willing to listen.

"Eddie said I had to prepare myself mentally because L.A. can be very distracting," Kobe said. "But I won't be doing a lot of hanging out after the games. I'll be going home to do homework and play video games, and, hopefully, chow down on a home-cooked meal. There will be time for fun, but right now I need to stay focused on basketball and get down to business. The only thing I want to do right now in L.A. is play and win a championship."

Inevitably, there were some distractions. Shortly after signing a three-year, $3.5 million contract with the Lakers, Kobe could be seen laughing it up with Jay Leno on *The Tonight Show*. He also escorted Brandy to the Hollywood premier of the movie *Eraser*. Endorsement opportunities were pouring in. None of this was surprising. Kobe was young, gifted, and charming. He was living in the entertainment capital of the world. It was only natural that his fame would quickly transcend the realm of sports.

Despite all the attention, Kobe tried not to take himself too seriously. Fortunately, he had help from the people closest to him: his family.

Not long after Kobe announced his intention to join the NBA, Joe Bryant resigned from his position as an assistant coach at La Salle. Joe was criticized in some circles for leaving the Explorers so that he could supposedly mastermind his son's career. Really, though, he was simply being a concerned parent. Kobe needed someone to help him sort out his options, and Joe was the perfect man for the job. The Bryants had always turned to each other for support and guidance, and that wasn't about to change simply because Kobe had become famous.

Similarly, they weren't about to let Kobe's new status as a professional basketball player splinter their family. When work obligations brought Joe Bryant to Italy in the early 1980s, the entire family had tagged along. Now that Kobe was relocating to the West Coast, it was time for mom and dad to follow their son.

After all, someone had to prepare all those "home-cooked meals."

"I'm really happy that my parents will be moving out with me," Kobe said. "We're a close family, and we've been together so long—living in Italy and other places—I would have definitely missed the support."

That summer Kobe bought a mansion in Pacific Palisades, a wealthy community near Los Angeles whose residents included actors Tom Cruise, Arnold Schwarzennegger, and Rosanne. Joe, Pam, and Shaya moved in with him. (Kobe's other sister, Sharia, who played volleyball at Temple, would join the family the next year, after she graduated.) Like any kid suddenly flush with money, Kobe splurged a little. He bought a few new cars for the family, including a Range Rover and a BMW. But for the most part he was cautious. During an Internet chat with young fans, Kobe was once asked what he planned to do with all his money. Very simply he said, "put it in the bank." Again, he was following the lead of his father. Joe Bryant had worked hard to save enough money to take care of his family. He had made smart investments. With the help of his family, Kobe planned to chart a similar course.

"When Kobe came onto the team, we said, 'Oh, my gosh, what are we going to have to do extra for this kid? How are we going to watch over him?'" Jerry West told the *Philadelphia Inquirer Magazine*. "But we haven't had to do anything. He's mature beyond his years, and he has his own clan with their own enclave in Pacific Palisades."

Wealth and fame did little to change life in the Bryant household. Kobe had a grown-up job with grown-up responsibilities, but in many ways he remained a kid. He had paid for the house by the ocean, and he had his own room filled with expensive electronic equipment. He was a budding superstar. To his parents and sisters, though, he was still just . . . *Kobe*. He was still part of the family.

"If Kobe goes out for a dinner after a game with friends, he calls and tells us where he is," Joe Bryant told the *Philadelphia Inquirer Magazine*. "If he goes somewhere from there, he calls again. We've been blessed. He's still a kid and a good kid. At home we still play and wrestle on the floor. We all climb on the same bed, watch a movie, and eat popcorn. It sounds corny, but that's what we do."

Kobe's combination of maturity and youthful enthusiasm made him an instant hit in Los Angeles. He charmed reporters and fans wherever he went. One question, however, remained: could he really play?

The answer wasn't long in coming. Less than a week after signing his first professional contract, Kobe began playing for the Lakers in the Fila Summer Pro League, an intensely competitive league featuring some of the best young players in the country. Kobe was the youngest of the young, but he wasn't even slightly intimidated. Just as he had in high school, he assumed a leadership role on the summer-league team. He routinely dispensed advice to teammates, directed them to specific spots on the floor, and generally acted like a much older, wiser player.

As he explained to a reporter from the *Los Angeles Times* one evening after scoring a game-high 36 points, "I just want to get out there and win. If the coach needs me to be a leader, that's what I'll be. And no matter what, if I see something wrong, I'm going to give my input, just like Shaq would give his input. But it's important for me to stay within the concept of the team."

Kobe's summer-league debut was nothing

short of sensational. With the Lakers' offense revolving around him, he averaged 25 points and 5.3 rebounds in four games. His presence naturally proved to be quite a boon to the Summer Pro League. The Long Beach Pyramid seats 5,000 fans, which is usually more than sufficient. But on the night that Kobe played his first game, the arena sold out early, and more than 2,000 fans were turned away. Those who were lucky enough to have seats witnessed quite a performance. Kobe, easily the most athletic and acrobatic player on the floor, scored 27 points in just 26 minutes.

Among the people impressed by Kobe that summer was Bob Lanier, who spent 15 years in the NBA and was inducted into the Hall of Fame in 1991. "He's got star written all over him," Lanier told the *Los Angeles Times* after watching Kobe play his final game. "He's got razzle-dazzle, personality, and he's flamboyant."

Everything about Kobe's first summer in Los Angeles led the Lakers to believe that they had made the right decision. He was adjusting quickly to his new surroundings, and he was obviously every bit as talented as Jerry West had suggested on draft day. The only time Kobe gave his new employers cause for concern was on September 2, when he broke his wrist while trying to dunk a ball during a pickup game at Venice Beach. Fortunately, the injury did not require surgery, which would have forced him to miss a substantial chunk of the season. As it was, Kobe would have to miss much of the Lakers' pre-season training camp. For a rookie, of course, that was a problem.

"This will set him back," Lakers general manager Mitch Kupchak said at the time. "He's an eighteen-year-old player and the first training camp is very important. If you're looking for a silver lining, it's that now we won't rush him along."

And, as another Laker official pointed out, it's hard to get mad at a kid who loves basketball so much that he goes looking for pickup games at the beach—even when he's a millionaire.

6

THE ROOKIE

On October 14, 1996, the Los Angeles Lakers conducted their annual media day at the Forum. The players strolled out onto the floor in full uniform and posed for photographs. They conducted endless interviews, answering the same questions over and over. One might have expected that the hulking presence of Shaquille O'Neal, sporting a Los Angeles uniform for the very first time, would draw the most attention. But that wasn't the case. Instead, the reporters gathered quickly around the team's youngest and most intriguing player.

Kobe Bryant.

Their interest stemmed not merely from the fact that the kid was about to break new ground by becoming the youngest player to appear in an NBA game. Or from the fact that he was already one of the most recognizable and popular athletes in Los Angeles. The reason everyone wanted to talk to Kobe was to find out how he was feeling.

It had been more than six weeks since his unfortunate tumble on the asphalt of Venice Beach. Kobe's wrist had healed right on schedule, but he had still missed a large chunk of training camp. In fact, in a few short hours, after the completion of media day, he would be taking part in his first full-contact practice session.

Still, some of the Lakers couldn't resist the urge to tease Kobe about his fame. At one point, Shaq saw Kobe surrounded by microphones and cameras and yelled out, "Hey, Showboat!" Kobe took the good-natured ribbing in stride. He'd been on the sideline long enough. Now all he wanted was a chance to test himself against some of the players he most admired. "I've been waiting to go out and compete with guys like Nick Van Exel and Eddie Jones," he said. "I'm really excited to have a chance to learn from them."

The Lakers were equally excited about seeing Kobe in action for the first time, and that afternoon he didn't disappoint. Practice went smoothly and Kobe fit in well. Best of all, his wrist seemed to be completely healed. "It felt fine. There was no pain at all," he told reporters afterward. "It felt great to be out there playing five on five again."

That news came as a relief to the Lakers' front office and coaching staff. With any young, athletically gifted player, there are going to be tense moments. Players who fly high and often, and who love to compete, are going to risk injury. Perhaps now, the Lakers' brass hoped, Kobe would be just a bit more cautious. They didn't want to dampen his enthusiasm, but they also didn't want him taking any unnecessary chances.

Unfortunately, it wasn't long before Kobe endured another crash landing. On October 18 the Lakers played their first home exhibition game of the season, against the Philadelphia 76ers. Kobe, naturally, was excited. Two nights earlier he had scored 10 points and grabbed five rebounds in his first professional game, helping the Lakers to a 90–80 victory over the Dallas Mavericks in a game played in Fresno, California. It was an impressive debut, but now he would be performing in L.A. for the first time, and that made the game just a bit more important.

There were more than 14,000 fans at the Forum that night, a good crowd for an exhibition game. They had come primarily to get a glimpse of the Lakers' newest acquisitions—Shaq and Kobe—and Kobe didn't want to let them down. He was also pumped because the opponent was a team from his hometown, a team that had once employed his father, Joe Bryant. Kobe had seen a lot of 76ers games as a kid. He had worked out with the team while he was in high school. He had something to prove in this game, even though he never would have admitted it.

The Lakers easily defeated the 76ers, 113–92. It was a typically ragged preseason affair—lots of turnovers, missed shots and sloppy defense. There were also a few breathtaking moments. Shaq was given a warm ovation when introduced, for instance, and Kobe brought the Forum crowd to its feet with an assortment of offensive moves, including two dunks.

He also prompted the loudest *Gasp!* of the evening when, with 4:26 remaining, he drove to the basket in his usual aggressive manner. As Kobe was quickly, and painfully, discovering he was no longer playing for Lower Merion High School. A few months earlier a move such as this would have split the defense and left an open lane to the basket. Not in the NBA. Suddenly everyone was bigger, stronger, faster. In high school Kobe had always been one of the biggest players on the floor. Now he found the basket protected by players who were six inches taller and 50 pounds heavier than he was. The paint was not a place for the timid or frail.

As Kobe sliced down the right side of lane, his path was blocked by Philadelphia center Tim Kempton. While in midair Kobe contorted his body wildly in an attempt to get off a clean shot, and smacked into Kempton. Kobe fell awkwardly and landed on his lower back. He stayed on the floor for a moment, then rose to his feet and walked gingerly off the court as the crowd applauded nervously. At that moment, Lakers fans had to wonder whether this was what Jerry West had meant when he said of Kobe, "During his first couple of seasons, you're going to see him do one or two things each game that will simply amaze you." One could only hope not. If he had to withstand many more collisions like this one, Kobe's career might not last a couple of seasons.

Kobe's injury was later diagnosed as a strained left hip flexor. The pain was so severe that he was forced to miss the team's next exhibition game against the Phoenix Suns, and his status was listed as "day to day." Kobe's apparent fragility naturally provided his critics with ammunition. The season hadn't even begun yet and already the kid had been injured twice. Maybe he really wasn't cut out for the NBA. Maybe his body could have used a few years of college ball. Maybe he had made a mistake.

Kobe scoffed at that notion, as did his teammates and coaches. They'd seen enough of Kobe in practice to know that he was right where he belonged. In time he would learn to choose his battles more carefully. Veteran players know when to drive to the basket and when to pull the ball out. They understand the risks associated with challenging a 275-pound center. They know that a bad decision can lead to a career-ending injury. Kobe, on the other hand, was the greenest of rookies—a raw but spirited 18-year-old kid who was accustomed to dunking over thick-legged converted soccer players. It really hadn't dawned on him that he might not be able to get away with some of those same moves in the NBA. And it certainly hadn't occurred to him that he might get seriously hurt in the process.

In time, his perception would change.

"Sometimes, you're better off with the three-foot bank," Kobe's friend, Eddie Jones, told reporters the day after Kobe was injured. "You've got to save yourself. You're going to get beat up enough going through screens and getting elbows. He's so young and so excited to be out there. And he wants to do something that will make the crowd 'ooh' and 'aah.' But he'll learn."

Kobe did not play another preseason game, and when the Lakers defeated the Phoenix Suns on opening night at the Forum, he never left the bench. On November 3, in a 91–85 victory over the Minnesota Timberwolves, Kobe finally got a chance to show what he could do—barely. He played just six minutes; his only shot was blocked. And he turned the ball over once. It was not exactly a memorable debut, except for the fact that it made Kobe the youngest player ever to appear in an NBA regular-season game.

But even that token would soon be taken away by Portland's Jermaine O'Neal, who also had jumped directly from high school to the NBA.

If anyone associated with the Lakers was upset about Kobe's slow start, they certainly didn't show it. As coach Del Harris said, "I'm sure he would have liked to make a more auspicious debut. It's OK. We already know he can play."

On November 6, the Lakers traveled to Charlotte for a game against the Hornets, the team that had originally drafted Kobe. Not surprisingly, there was some animosity on the part of Charlotte's fans, who had expected Kobe to be playing in their city full-time. Months earlier there had been wild speculation about the reasons behind the trade. In truth, the Lakers wanted Kobe and the Hornets were merely using him as trade bait. But Kobe's agent, Arn Tellem, had stirred up controversy by implying shortly after the draft that Kobe would only play for the Lakers. Now, more than four months later, basketball fans in Charlotte still resented Kobe and what they perceived to be his agent's strong-armed tactics. When asked to reflect on the negotiations that took him from Charlotte to Los Angeles, Kobe told the *Charlotte Observer*, "I'm in the NBA—I was never worried about where it would be."

Nevertheless, Kobe expected to be treated unkindly when he returned to Charlotte, and he wasn't mistaken. The crowd of 24,042 at Charlotte Coliseum serenaded Kobe with a chorus of boos when he entered the game late in the first half and continued to boo each time he touched the ball. Overall, though, Hornets fans didn't have much reason to be unhappy. Kobe had three turnovers in just seven minutes of playing time as Charlotte handed the Lakers their first defeat of the season, 88–78.

The maturity that impressed so many NBA scouts and executives helped carry Kobe through those early games. Although his playing time was severely restricted, he never complained, never hung his head, a fact that impressed Del Harris. "Kobe is pretty sophisticated for an 18-year-old," the coach told the Associated Press. "His dad spent eight years in the NBA and eight years in Europe, and Kobe was with him. He's been around the pro basketball scene, and that's one reason why it might work out better for him than it would for some other 18-year-olds."

The Lakers got off to a good start in the 1996–97 season, winning eight of their first 11 games. Shaq was adjusting well to his new team. Eddie Jones was his usual smooth self. And Nick Van Exel seemed more confident than ever at point guard. For Kobe Bryant, however, everything was a struggle. He found the transition from high school to professional basketball to be enormously challenging and frequently frustrating. In the Lakers' first nine games he played a grand total of just 59 minutes. Although he was never fearful or tentative, he was often out of control. Perhaps because he wanted so badly to stay in the game, Kobe would often try to make something happen, even if no opportunity was available. The predictable results were turnovers and fouls.

In the tenth game of the season, against the winless Phoenix Suns, Kobe finally played the way he knew he was capable of playing. Although he played only 14 minutes, he made the most of each second on the floor. On this night, almost everything went right for Kobe. He hit four of six three-point shots and finished with 16 points, second only to Jones (18) for team scoring honors, as the Lakers rolled to a 102–88 victory.

It was a performance that pleased not only Kobe, but his teammates and coach, as well. If anyone was under more pressure than Kobe, it was Del Harris, for it was his job to bring Kobe along at the proper pace. Many Lakers fans, caught up in a wave of Kobe hysteria, wanted to see the rookie playing 40 minutes a game right from the start. Harris knew that wasn't realistic. On this night he saw flashes of the star that Kobe seemed destined to become. But everyone, including Kobe, would have to be patient.

"I was very happy with Kobe," Harris told

reporters after the game. "He made a couple of turnovers, but he was terrific. Being a competitive guy, he's impatient and he gets frustrated. You can just tell with his body language and some of his expressions and such. It's understandable. As he comes out and grows through his mistakes, he will get playing time based on how he does."

The coach wasn't unsympathetic to the young superstar's ambition. But he did have a responsibility to the franchise and its fans to make sure that Kobe wasn't given minutes he hadn't really earned. Sometimes, though, the coach was compelled to use Kobe, whether the kid was ready or not. One such occasion occurred on November 26, in Philadelphia of all places.

The game was billed as a homecoming for Kobe and Eddie Jones, the two buddies from Philly, and neither player denied that it meant a little more than the usual contest. On the flight from Los Angeles to Philadelphia, Jones would later divulge, he and Bryant had promised each other that they would put on a show that the hometown fans would never forget. That Jones held up his end of the bargain by scoring 23 points and recording a career-high eight steals was no great surprise—more and more, he was looking like an NBA All-Star. But who would have guessed that Kobe would be thrust into such an important role and respond so impressively?

In such demand for interviews that he had to conduct a special pregame press conference, Kobe then went out and played a season-high 21 minutes. When the Lakers experienced foul trouble in the first quarter, Harris turned to his bench and inserted three rookies—Kobe, Derek Fisher and Travis Knight—into the game. All three played well enough to keep the Lakers close, and Kobe did much more. He scored all 12 of his points in the second quarter as the Lakers took the lead and cruised to a 100–88 victory.

Just as quickly as his star seemed to be rising, though, it fell again. Twice in the first week of December Kobe watched entire games from the bench. Physically, he was fine. He was hungry to play. But when the Lakers found themselves in tight games, Harris repeatedly chose not to use his talented rookie. The reason: Kobe was still making too many mistakes. This was a completely foreign experience to Kobe. Not since sixth grade had a coach kept him on the bench for an entire game. He didn't like it then, and he didn't like it now. Still, he rarely betrayed any emotion about the subject. He desperately wanted more playing time, but if the Lakers felt he needed to sharpen his game, then that's what he would do.

"I just have to be real patient," Kobe told the *Los Angeles Times*. "Just keep working on my game. That's what I'm trying to do."

The first half of the season was a roller-coaster—there were some terrible days, and there were some very good days. On January 28, for example, he became the youngest player in NBA history to start a regular-season game. For Kobe, it was a nice emotional lift heading into the All-Star Break. In a few days he would be participating in the event's annual rookie game, as well as the slam-dunk contest. There, he thought, he'd have a chance to strut his stuff. He had no idea how right he was.

7

IN YOUR FACE!

All-Star Weekend is the NBA's mid-season carnival. The best players in the league gather in one city for a series of events designed to showcase their athleticism and charisma. It's a fan-friendly weekend that includes plenty of time for interviews and autographs, as well as a sensational display of basketball.

The premier attraction is Sunday afternoon's All-Star Game, which pits the best players from the Western Conference against the best players from the Eastern Conference. Fans vote on the starting lineups for both squads; the remaining players are selected by the league's coaches. In 1997, the Lakers placed two players on the West squad: Shaquille O'Neal and Eddie Jones. Shaq, unfortunately, was forced to miss the game because of a sprained knee. But Jones played impressively in his All-Star debut, scoring 10 points in a 132–120 loss to the East.

The atmosphere at Cleveland's Gund Arena that February weekend was electric, thanks largely to the presence of many of the NBA's legendary performers. As part of the league's fiftieth anniversary celebration, the NBA honored its fifty greatest players during a special ceremony at half-time of the All-Star Game. Among the honorees were no less than *eight* current or former Los Angeles Lakers: Shaquille O'Neal, Wilt Chamberlain, Jerry West, George Mikan, Elgin Baylor, Kareem Abdul-Jabbar, Magic Johnson, and James Worthy. All were in attendance, and their presence reminded everyone that the Lakers were indeed one of the most successful franchises in sports history.

With Shaq and Eddie Jones still in their early twenties, there was no reason to think the team would be sliding to the bottom of the league's pecking order anytime soon. Shaq, obviously, was already a superstar, and Jones was among the most respected young players in the league. Together they had led the Lakers to a Pacific Division-leading record of 35–13 at the All-Star break. But they represented only part of the reason for optimism. Another indication of the Lakers' potential for dominance was on display earlier in the weekend, in the All-Star Rookie Game and the Slam Dunk Championship. His name was Kobe Bryant.

*   *   *

Saturday, February 8, was a remarkably busy day for Kobe. Despite the fact that he wasn't really even an All-Star, he was among the most sought-after players at Gund Arena. Fans—especially young fans—wanted his autograph. Reporters wanted interviews. Then there was the matter of playing a little basketball. Kobe was one of sixteen players invited to participate in the Rookie Game, a showcase for the NBA's future stars, on Saturday afternoon. His West teammates, in addition to fellow Lakers Derek Fisher and Travis Knight, included Shareef Abdur-Rahim, a versatile forward from the Vancouver Grizzlies; Matt Maloney, a sharpshooting guard from the Houston Rockets; and Steve Nash, a ball-handling wizard from the Phoenix Suns. Point guard Stephon Marbury of the Minnesota Timberwolves, another of the league's brightest prospects, had been invited to play but was sidelined with an injury. Coaching the team was Red Holzman, a member of the NBA Hall of Fame who had guided the New York Knicks to a pair of NBA titles in the early 1970s.

The East squad had even more talent, including Allen Iverson, a point guard from the Philadelphia 76ers with a devastating, ankle-breaking crossover dribble; Marcus Camby, a center from the Toronto Raptors who had been the national college player of the year at the University of Massachusetts; Antoine Walker, a muscular forward from the Boston Celtics; and

Kerry Kittles, a smooth guard from the New Jersey Nets. Coaching the East was another "Red"—Red Auerbach, perhaps the greatest coach in basketball history, and the man who was at the helm when the Boston Celtics ruled the NBA in the 1950s and 1960s.

To many observers, the Rookie Game could be distilled into one great match-up: a duel between Kobe Bryant and Allen Iverson, two of the league's most explosive and exciting young guards. And that's precisely what it turned out to be.

Kobe was clearly the fan favorite. Iverson, a startlingly quick guard with the lean build of a sprinter, was having a sensational year and was on his way to being named NBA Rookie of the Year. But his approach to the game offended some purists. Although he was a point guard, and therefore primarily responsible for running the 76ers offense and getting his teammates involved, Iverson was often the team's leading scorer. He took a lot of shots; sometimes he took bad shots. He also turned the ball over frequently. There was no denying that Iverson, with his incredible ball-handling skills and darting moves to the basket, was one of the game's most entertaining players. But he had also been criticized for his apparent selfishness, and for a brazen attitude that seemed to border on arrogance.

So, it was no great surprise that the crowd at

Gund Arena showered Iverson with boos during the Rookie Game, even though his performance was dazzling. Iverson did, however, make a few new fans on this day, including his coach. "The kid is coachable," Auerbach said. "With all of his flair and flamboyance, he's coachable. I love him. He's a very attentive kid."

Iverson, the number one pick in the 1996 NBA draft, finished the game with 19 points and nine assists in leading the East to a 96–91 victory. The only person whose performance was superior to Iverson's was Kobe Bryant. With the East holding a 51–36 halftime lead, Kobe decided to take matters into his own hands. Using an assortment of gravity-defying moves, along with a deft touch from the foul line (he made 13 of 16 free throws), Kobe nearly brought the West back. The rally ultimately fell short, but Kobe finished with a game-high 31 points.

While Iverson was jeered throughout the afternoon, Kobe was cheered wildly. In the end, the MVP trophy went to Iverson, primarily because the MVP trophy almost always goes to a member of the winning team. But even Iverson had to admit that Kobe's performance was stunning.

"Kobe played a great game," Iverson said. "I think he's been great all year. The guy never even played college basketball."

Nope. Not a minute of college ball. But as

the Rookie Game proved, Kobe's classmates had
nothing on him. Teenager or not, he fit right in.

In Kobe's case, there was little rest for the weary.
On Saturday evening, just a few short hours
after the Rookie Game, he stepped back onto the
floor at Gund Arena. This was what he'd been
waiting for—an opportunity to express not only
his raw athleticism but his creativity as well. It
was time for the Slam Dunk Championship.

"There's nothing like it," Kobe would later
say during an interview with ESPN. "You get a
chance to put on a show in front of the players
that you idolized growing up, the players who
made the league what it is today. I watched the
competition every year, from Dr. J, David
Thompson, Michael Jordan on."

Dr. J . . . David Thompson . . . Michael Jor-
dan . . .

Three of the greatest aerial artists the game
of basketball has ever known—and three of the
men responsible for making the Slam Dunk
Championship a fan favorite at All-Star
Weekend. The event was actually born in the
winter of 1976, when the American Basketball
Association staged the first slam dunk contest at
Denver's McNichols Arena. The ABA was con-
ceived as a flashy alternative to the stodgy NBA.
The new league featured a red-white-and-blue
basketball and a shameless run-and-gun philoso-

phy. It might have been a triumph of style over substance, but there was no denying its ability to entertain. In this atmosphere a slam dunk contest seemed to make perfect sense.

The ABA might not have had as much talent as the NBA, but it did have a number of gifted players in 1976, including David "Skywalker" Thompson of the Denver Nuggets and Dr. J—the legendary Julius Erving—of the New York Nets. Dr. J was the first of the game's great leapers, a player who glided effortlessly above defenses. He was the favorite at the first slam dunk contest, and he more than lived up to his reputation. Erving brought the crowd at McNichols Arena to its feet with his winning move. He sprinted the length of the floor, took off from the foul line, and slammed the ball through the hoop! No one had ever seen anything like it . . . but they would certainly recognize it years down the road, when future slam dunk champions Michael Jordan and Brent Barry copied Dr. J's signature move.

The ABA staged just one slam dunk contest and soon went out of business, although many of its top players, and some of its teams, were absorbed by the NBA. In 1984 the NBA smartly resurrected the event, and the Slam Dunk Championship quickly became a staple of All-Star Weekend. Larry Nance, a 6–10 center for the Phoenix Suns, won the first contest by cradling the ball between his palm and forearm, rocking it back and forth in midair, and then throwing down a thunderous reverse dunk. It was a sensational move, flawlessly executed, and just enough to lift Nance over the sentimental favorite, Julius Erving.

Over the course of the next dozen years the NBA Slam Dunk Championship featured an assortment of memorable performances: 5-foot–7 Spud Webb of the Atlanta Hawks outjumping and outdunking 6-foot–8 teammate Dominique Wilkins in 1986; Michael Jordan winning back-to-back titles in 1987 and 1988; Cedric Ceballos of the Phoenix Suns wearing a blindfold in 1992; and Brent Barry paying tribute to Dr. J, who also happened to be one of the judges, in 1996.

Erving was back at the judges table in 1997, along with retired NBA superstars George Gervin, Walt Frazier, and Bob Lanier, and current WNBA star Lisa Leslie. A student of basketball history, Kobe was familiar with the résumés of each of the judges. But it was the presence of Dr. J, who was once a teammate of Joe Bryant's on the Philadelphia 76ers, that most excited him.

"It feels great to get a guy like Dr. J out of his seat," Kobe would tell ESPN after the contest. "He's the guy who's made all this possible. He played in Philadelphia with my father, and he's seen me grow up."

By 1997 the Slam Dunk Championship was no longer attracting the league's marquee players. The risk of injury was simply too great, and the potential payoff ($20,000) too small—at least, too small for a player who earns several million dollars annually. So in recent years the contest had featured younger, hungrier players. In addition to Kobe, the lineup in 1997 included Chris Carr of the Minnesota Timberwolves, Michael Finley of the Dallas Mavericks, Darvin Ham of the Denver Nuggets, and Bob Sura of the Cleveland Cavaliers.

Sura, a rookie guard out of Florida State, was the hometown favorite. Unfortunately, he failed to advance out of the first round. Ham and Allen also were eliminated. Kobe, meanwhile, was the last player to qualify for the final. He edged Hamm by just one point in the first round, and his performance hardly indicated that he was poised to capture the slam dunk title. But he was.

In the final, each player was allowed to attempt two dunks. The panel of five judges graded each dunk on a scale of one to 10, making 50 the highest possible score. Each player in the final was allowed to keep the better of his two dunks.

Kobe had followed the Slam Dunk Championship since he was a kid—he'd even participated in a similar event when he was a high school senior—so he understood that soaring high and far wasn't enough. In any slam dunk contest, *style* is the key. And Kobe had style. On the first of his two dunks he galloped in from the left wing, leaped high into the air, passed the ball between his legs, from his left hand to his right hand . . . and threw down a ferocious, rim-shaking windmill jam!

It was an incredible dunk, one that could have gone wrong in about five different places. Anything less than perfect execution and timing would have resulted in Kobe missing spectacularly—and embarrassingly. It was, to say the least, a high-risk maneuver. But he pulled it off. As Kobe landed, the crowd roared in approval. The judges, including Dr. J, threw their hands in the air in disbelief.

But Kobe wasn't quite through. There was still time to put a little icing on this cake. As Gund Arena shook with applause, Kobe strutted to the sideline and faced a throng of NBA All-Stars past and present. He then pursed his lips and flexed his muscles like a bodybuilder. The crowd ate it up. So did the All-Stars.

"Man, that part was sweet," said Miami Heat center Alonzo Mourning, echoing the sentiments of the judges, who awarded Kobe a near-perfect score of 49.

"The crowd got me real pumped up after the dunk, and I just felt like flexing," Kobe explained. "I don't have much, but I flexed what I have. I don't do that kind of stuff in a game, only in a dunking competition."

Kobe missed his second dunk, but it really didn't matter. His first slam had already put enormous pressure on the rest of the field. Carr responded with an impressive 360-degree jam off a high bounce pass, but the judges awarded him only 45 points for the effort, perhaps because he simply wasn't as animated as Kobe had been. "I was a little disappointed," Carr said. "I thought that was a pretty difficult dunk. But they get paid to judge and I get paid to dunk."

Even more difficult was the acrobatic move attempted by Michael Finley. An inventive, highly athletic player, Finley tried to dunk the ball after completing a cartwheel. It was one of the most original moves ever attempted in the Slam Dunk Championship, and had it been successful, Finley might well have walked off with first prize. As it turned out, though, Finley missed both of his dunks in the final round, and Kobe became the NBA's newest slam dunk champion.

For Kobe, the slam dunk title was a sweet conclusion to a long, challenging day. It also eased the disappointment that he had to have felt after not being named MVP of the Rookie Game, despite playing so well. "Both of them would have been nice," Kobe admitted afterward. "I was psyched for the dunk contest as it was, but [not being MVP] brought me up a little bit more."

Before leaving Cleveland, Kobe vowed to defend his title the next year. He didn't care about the danger, and he didn't care about the money.

He just loved to fly . . . and to perform. He couldn't have known then that the NBA would abolish the Slam Dunk Championship, thereby robbing him of an opportunity to make good on that promise. For one day, though, eighteen-year-old Kobe Bryant was the NBA's emperor of the air.

8

LESSONS LEARNED

In the wake of his captivating performance at NBA All-Star Weekend, Kobe saw his popularity soar. His flying and flexing had been the centerpiece of every sports highlight show in the country for days afterward, and the fallout was obvious. No longer just a prodigy who might eventually grow into his talent, he was now seen as a true showman. On the NBA's calendar of events, only the playoffs have a higher profile than All-Star Weekend. To a lot of young basketball fans, who consider the ability to slam and style the ultimate measure of a player's worth, Kobe was king of the court. He was charming, good-looking, smart; he seemed to have wings.

Best of all, at eighteen years of age, he was practically one of them—a kid. He shared their taste in fashion, movies, and music. Like them, he was a hip-hop kid. He was even an accomplished rapper!

With this new level of celebrity came a heavy

dose of responsibility. Not that Kobe minded. Unlike a lot of professional athletes, he understood that fame and wealth came at a price. That was just one of the lessons he had learned while growing up. His every move would be watched closely, especially by the young fans who admired him most, kids who were now rushing out to buy his signature shoe, the Adidas KB8. If he screwed up, he would disappoint a lot of people. Like it or not, he was a role model.

"I think that's really cool," Kobe told the *Long Beach Press Telegram.* "I love kids myself. I feel very comfortable around them. Hey, I'm still a kid myself. I think one reason a lot of the kids like me is that they can relate to me. I think a lot of the kids cheering for me these days are people only four, five, six years younger than me.

"I guess it's an added responsibility for me to be looked up to, but I'll take it. It doesn't bother me a bit. I'll just continue to try to be myself."

Unfortunately for Kobe, while that refreshingly mature, responsible attitude served him well off the court, it wasn't enough to ensure success in the NBA. The fact remained that Kobe was just eighteen years old and was still having trouble adjusting to the intensely competitive nature of professional basketball. In high school everything had come easily to him. He was usually the best ball handler on the floor, the best outside shooter, and the best rebounder. Even though his high school coach had tried to involve his Lower Merion teammates in the offense, everyone understood that it was Kobe's team. In a pinch they could simply hand him the ball and clear out of the way.

In the NBA, that rarely worked for the best players, and it sure wasn't going to work for an eighteen-year-old rookie. Too often Kobe resorted to the simple offensive philosophy that had carried him through high school: *Go ahead—try to stop me.* His slashing, acrobatic moves to the basket often provoked oohs and aahs from the fans at the Great Western Forum, but they resulted in turnovers and missed shots as often as they resulted in points. Kobe had to learn that while it was okay to demonstrate a flair for the dramatic in slam dunk contests and all-star games, there was little room for such theatrics within the confines of the real world. Or, as Nick Van Exel put it, Kobe had to rein in his tendency to play "one-on-five."

For the most part, the rest of the Lakers were tolerant of Kobe's occasional hotdogging. They understood that it stemmed largely from his youthful exuberance. No one wanted to squeeze the raw enthusiasm out of Kobe—that, after all, was what fueled him. The trick was to find a way to harness all that energy and ability, to make it fit neatly into a team concept. The Lakers had more talent than any other team in the league. Kobe had to be patient. He had to learn that it simply wasn't necessary to do everything by himself.

Kobe's entire rookie year was one long tutorial, the Great Western Forum his classroom. Like any student who has been pushed ahead a few grades, he had his good moments and bad moments. On some nights he displayed flashes of brilliance. He was so quick, so smooth, so confident that he would leave his teammates practically awestruck. "It's going to be scary when he's 24, 25, 26 years old," Shaquille O'Neal told *People* magazine. "It's going to be real scary."

In an interview with *Courtside* magazine, Kurt Rambis, a Lakers assistant coach (and former player), echoed O'Neal's thoughts. Rambis called Kobe "the complete package. He's going to be a great, great ball player because he has all the physical tools, the work ethic, and the competitiveness. His big thing now is mental, working within the system, letting the system do things for him instead of doing it himself. He's learning to move without the ball, when to go one-on-one, when to pass. It comes with time and maturity. And consistency will come with learning and listening to us. He had a style of play from high school which we tried to drastically change. He wants to be coached, even though it gets him frustrated. In the back of his mind, he wants help.

"Michael Jordan had to do the same thing," Rambis added. "He wanted to do it himself, but he learned when to get his teammates involved.

It's a long process. For some players it can take eight years. We hope, for Kobe's sake, it's a short process."

No one was more anxious to see Kobe develop than Lakers head coach Del Harris, for it was he who had been assigned the task of schooling the young superstar. Harris was in a very difficult position. The Lakers had invested a lot of money in Kobe, and they wanted a return on their investment as quickly as possible. Fans who came to the Forum wanted to see number eight in action. So there was pressure on Harris to make sure that Kobe got plenty of playing time. On the other hand, as the team's head coach, his primary responsibility was to make sure that the Lakers won as many games as they were capable of winning. Those two objectives— minutes for Kobe and a potential NBA championship—were often at odds with each other. After all, Harris couldn't reward Kobe for playing recklessly or selfishly. If he did that, the other players would get angry. They'd lose respect for the coach. Worse, the Lakers would lose more games than they won.

Harris decided that Kobe would have to earn his minutes just like everyone else. If that meant the coach would sometimes hear boos from the Forum crowd, so be it. If he'd occasionally be summoned to the general manager's office for a little chat about the progress of Kobe Bryant, well, he could handle that, too.

"Kobe's showboating frustrates his team-mates," Harris said during a 1997 interview with the *New York Times Magazine.* "He may see me as the first real obstacle in his life. The first adult who told him he was wrong. I don't want to be remembered like that. The guy who wouldn't let Kobe play. But I have to do it. I can't give him special treatment just because he's eighteen. He elected to come into a man's world, and he'll have to play by a man's rules."

Even as his fame and popularity were spreading, Kobe was feeling the backlash that so often comes with being a prodigy. Expectations are enormous, and a certain percentage of the population wants to see you fail. As Kobe was shifted from shooting guard to point guard to small forward and then back to shooting guard in the first two months of 1997, he began to flounder. The comfort that he had always felt on the basketball court disappeared. He seemed, for the first time, unsure of himself; at times he appeared almost lost.

Every athlete experiences a slump from time to time, but this was all new to Kobe. He tried to regain his confidence by playing more aggressively, by attacking the basket. But that was precisely what Harris did not want him to do. He wanted Kobe to understand his role. He wanted Kobe to watch . . . and learn.

Predictably, as Kobe's minutes dwindled in late February and March, criticism began to

mount. Perhaps, some observers wondered, the
kid had made a mistake after all. A particularly
harsh *New York Times Magazine* article painted
a portrait of the artist as a young sham—a kid
unprepared both physically and emotionally for
the rigors of the NBA. In *People* magazine,
respected NBC basketball analyst Peter Vecsey
was quoted as saying that Del Harris "is questioning Bryant's commitment and attitude." He
added, somewhat sympathetically, "It's tough for
a kid right out of high school to understand that
if you don't play, you can't sulk."

If Kobe was pouting, it sure wasn't obvious.
As he told *LA Sports Profiles,* "Sometimes you
might get a little down because you want to go
out there and contribute to the team. But I just
keep looking at the long-term goals and keep
working hard every day so that when my time is
called, I can go out there and contribute."

As February gave way to March, opportuni-
ties for Kobe to contribute were rare. He usually
played only a few minutes per night; sometimes
he didn't play at all. Not only was this bad for
Kobe, it was bad for the Lakers. With Shaquille
O'Neal still recovering from a torn ligament in
his knee, Harris struggled to find a consistently
productive lineup. By early April, with the playoffs on the horizon, Van Exel and Jones were
also hurting. If the Lakers were to be successful
in post-season play, they would have to get more
help off the bench. That meant Kobe Bryant

would have to polish his game—in a hurry.

On April 8, in a game against the Golden State Warriors, the Lakers finally got the kind of bench production they would need if they hoped to make a run at an NBA championship. The Lakers' reserves scored an NBA season-high 70 points in a 109–85 victory. Not since 1990 had the team gotten such offensive firepower from its bench, and the person leading the way was . . . Kobe Bryant.

In his best all-around game of the season, Kobe made nine of eleven shots from the floor and scored a team-high 24 points as the Lakers moved into a tie for first place in the Pacific Division. And he did it while backing up Derek Fisher at point guard. This was wonderful news for the Lakers, who might need Kobe at any one of three positions in the playoffs. That he played so well in an important game—a game with play-off implications—was another good sign. Kobe had always been cool under pressure. Maybe, somehow, he would not get rattled during his first trip to the NBA playoffs.

Then again, maybe he was just too naive to understand what this all meant.

"He has no idea," veteran guard Byron Scott told reporters after the game. "He's just playing and having fun and enjoying himself. He knows he wants to win a championship, but I don't think he knows all the stuff that goes with it."

Soon enough, he'd find out.

On the final day of the regular season the Lakers lost to the Portland Trail Blazers, 100–95. The defeat cost them the Pacific Division title, but they still wound up with a 56–26 record, their best mark in seven years. In his rookie season, Kobe averaged 7.6 points, 1.9 rebounds, and 1.3 assists. He played 15.5 minutes per game. Those numbers were good enough to earn a spot on the NBA All-Rookie Second team, along with teammate Travis Knight. But the season had been such a roller coaster that it was almost impossible to guess how Kobe would perform in the playoffs.

He started out slowly. In a first-round match-up against the Trail Blazers, Kobe played a total of just six minutes in the first two games as the Lakers jumped out to a 2–0 lead. In Game 3, a disappointing 98–90 loss, Kobe came off the bench to score 22 points and was one of the team's few bright spots. "He was able to create, penetrate, get in there and get a foul," noted Nick Van Exel, who spent much of the game on the bench. "He has a knack for getting fouled, for getting to the free-throw line. I noticed one thing about Kobe. He was aggressive. Nobody else was. By the time we got to looking at the scoreboard, we were already twenty down. We needed what he gave us."

In Game 4, however, Kobe went back to the bench. He played a total of just 39 minutes in the series and was held scoreless in three of the four games. Despite his limited input, the Lakers eliminated the Trail Blazers, three games to one, thanks largely to an awesome performance by Shaquille O'Neal. Obviously fully recovered from his knee injury, Shaq averaged 33 points and 9.2 rebounds. He also blocked seven shots. Shaq was at his most dominant on the first night of the series, when he scored 46 points—the most points tallied by a Laker in the playoffs since Jerry West had 53 against the Boston Celtics in 1969.

In the Western Conference semifinals the Lakers faced a far more daunting opponent: the Utah Jazz. With a lineup anchored by two sure Hall of Famers, point guard John Stockton and power forward Karl Malone, the Jazz were one of the most talented and experienced teams in the NBA. If the Lakers were to have any chance in this series, they would have to be at their very best. They'd have to play with a consistency and a level of intensity they'd shown only periodically during the regular season.

Game 1 at the Delta Center in Salt Lake City, Utah, didn't exactly boost the confidence of Lakers fans, as the Jazz rolled to a 93–77 victory. Game 2 was a vast improvement—Shaq had 25 points and Robert Horry set an NBA post-season record for most three-pointers in a game without a miss (he made all seven of his attempts)—but the Lakers still came out on the short end of a 103–101 decision.

For Game 3, the series moved to Los Angeles. Comfortable in their own surroundings, the Lakers hammered the Jazz, 104–84, behind a surprisingly self-assured performance by Kobe, who made 13 of 14 free throws and finished with a team-high 19 points, including 17 in the fourth quarter. By playing so well, the Lakers had not only avoided a sweep, they had at least temporarily given an indication that the series might turn out to be a true battle. Game 4, however, belonged to Karl Malone. A bruising 6–9, 250-pound forward with a ferocious appetite for competition, Malone is one of the greatest players in the history of the NBA, especially in pressure situations. On this day he scored 42 points to give the Jazz a 110–95 victory and what appeared to be an insurmountable 3–1 lead in the best-of-seven series.

Worst of all for the Lakers, Game 5 would be played at the Delta Center, home of the loudest fans in the NBA. As Kobe once observed, "In Utah the fans are right on top of you."

On May 12, they were in fine voice. The Delta Center rocked from the opening tip, and the Jazz naturally fed off the crowd's energy. The Lakers had to contend with this formidable sixth man while playing without one of their top reserves, Byron Scott, who was out with a sprained wrist. That was bad enough. Making matters worse was the loss of Robert Horry, who was ejected with 8:51 left in the third quarter after tussling with Utah's Jeff Hornacek. Malone, who finished with 32 points and 20 rebounds, made both free throws to give the Jazz a commanding 62–51 lead.

But the Lakers didn't quit. By the end of the quarter they had trimmed the deficit to just five points, and they continued to rally in the fourth quarter. With 9:24 left in the game, L.A. took a 69–68 lead, and the momentum seemed to be shifting. With 1:46 remaining, though, Shaq picked up his sixth personal foul and headed for the bench. If the Lakers were going to keep the series alive, they would have to do it without their best player.

Remarkably, they nearly pulled it off. With 39 seconds left the score was tied, 87–87. Eddie Jones slithered through traffic in the lane and got off a tough shot, but the ball was blocked by Utah's seven-foot center, Greg Ostertag. Moments later the Jazz had a chance to take the lead, but Malone's fadeaway jumper over three L.A. defenders rattled off the rim. Ostertag scooped up the rebound but was stripped by Van Exel, who called time-out with 11.3 seconds remaining in the game.

The Lakers jogged to their bench and listened intently to Harris. They watched closely as he drew up one final play. To the surprise of just about everyone at the Delta Center, and to millions more watching on network television, the coach called Kobe Bryant's number. In the most pressure-filled moment of the entire season, the ball would be in the hands of a rookie.

Kobe dribbled up the floor. With his team-mates spread out, trying to give him room to make a move, he finally pulled up and took a 14-foot jump shot that fell short. As the Delta Center crowd roared, the buzzer sounded, sending the game into overtime. Later, when pressed by reporters to explain why he had picked Kobe to take the last shot, Harris said simply, "He's an excellent one-on-one player. I'd give him that shot again anytime."

As it turned out, Kobe got several more attempts before the night was through. Three times in overtime he pulled up for long, difficult jump shots, and each time the ball caught nothing but air. The Lakers made just one of 10 shots in overtime. Without Shaq in the middle, they were unable to bang with Ostertag and Malone. Slowly, steadily, the Jazz pulled away. The final score was 98–93.

It was a painful way to end the season, especially for Kobe. He'd been given a remarkable opportunity—a chance to be the hero of an NBA playoff game at an age when most kids are finishing up their first year in college. But he also had been asked to shoulder a tremendous burden. "He's a young guy, and this is all new to him," Utah's John Stockton said sympathetically after the game. "He's played with a lot of confidence in this series, but he was asked to make some tough shots at the end, and he just didn't come up with them."

Down the hall, in another part of the Delta Center, Kobe Bryant sat quietly in front of his locker. Just about everyone seemed willing to cut the kid some slack. Teammates patted him on the back. Reporters took great care to phrase their questions delicately. But there was no consoling Kobe. He stared blankly into space, his mind someplace else. Already he was thinking about the next season, and how he would write a different ending.

9

SECOND SEASON,
SECOND CHANCES

On the flight from Salt Lake City to Los Angeles following Game 5 of the Western Conference semifinals, Kobe had time to think. He replayed that 14-foot shot at the end of regulation over and over in his mind. He thought about the air balls in overtime. He thought about what he might have done differently. Kobe had always been a student of the game; he knew that there was no shame in failing a test—so long as you gave your best effort and learned from your mistakes.

Many athletes would have wallowed in self-pity following an episode such as this. Not Kobe. By the time the Lakers' jet touched down in Los Angeles at two in the morning, he was already eager to begin patching the holes in his game. He drove to his home in Pacific Palisades and grabbed a few hours of fitful sleep. Early the next morning he jumped out of bed, threw on his workout gear, and drove to nearby Palisades High

School. Kobe had secured a set of keys to the gym so that he could play whenever the mood struck him—day or night—and this was just such an occasion. The Lakers would not be conducting formal practice sessions for several more months. Most of the players would take a few weeks to rest and recover, to let the bumps and bruises of a brutal NBA season heal.

Not Kobe. For more than three hours on the morning of May 13, he played shadow ball. He took hundreds of jump shots, firing over and over, until his arms ached and sweat rolled off his chin. When quizzed about this workout several months later, Kobe denied that it was some form of self-imposed punishment for having missed a game-winning shot. He was just playing a little ball, the way he did every morning. But as Jerry West told the *Philadelphia Inquirer,* "You can be sure he went to that same spot and started shooting."

West, who knew a little something about the pursuit of excellence, said this with a chuckle, for he understood what it meant. Most people looked at Kobe Bryant and saw a charming, happy-go-lucky kid with an easy laugh and athletic ability that seemed to come from another world. They saw a kid who just enjoyed playing basketball, having fun; a kid who had a smile that could light up the Forum, much as Magic Johnson's had a decade earlier. But West saw something else, something that was shared by all the great players, including Magic. He saw within Kobe a burning desire to be the best. He saw a fiercely competitive young man who hated losing—at anything.

The morning-after workout at Palisades High was just the beginning of a program that would help transform Kobe into one of the top players in the NBA. He returned the next morning to shoot several hundred more shots. And the morning after that. While many players, including some of his teammates, were taking a few weeks of vacation, Kobe was hard at work. Although to him it didn't really seem like work. He couldn't imagine stuffing his game in a closet for a while and hanging out on the beach. The thought of burnout never entered his mind.

"I can't do that," he told the *Orange County Register.* "I'd feel uncomfortable if I took a week off. I just want to play. I'd feel uncomfortable if I didn't play, didn't touch a basketball. When it's something you love to do, I can't see getting run-down doing it."

As much as he loved basketball, and as talented as he was, he also knew he would have to become bigger and stronger to compete successfully against the grown men he was facing in the NBA. His rookie year had taught him that much. So during the spring and summer of 1997, Kobe worked harder than he had ever worked in his life. Under the supervision of a personal trainer, Kobe embraced a world-class fitness regimen that would leave most athletes begging for mercy. Six days a week he would drive to a local track and run a series of gut-busting wind sprints. And that was just for a warm-up. Next he would travel to Gold's Gym for a few hours of weight training, followed by two hours of solitary work on his jump shot. Finally, late in the afternoon, he would head over to UCLA to play pickup ball against the best college and professional players in the Los Angeles area. Typically, he worked out for seven or eight hours a day. One day a week, at his trainer's insistence, he rested so that his body could recover.

As for the famously fast-paced L.A. lifestyle that has been known to distract even the most dedicated of athletes? Kobe wanted no part of it. He was more inclined to hang out at home. His idea of a big night was a pizza and a movie with his family. "I'm not the type of person who has a lot of friends," Kobe once said. "The friends I have, I basically have known my entire life. I don't go out looking for new friends. There are a lot of fake people out there, wherever you go. You just have to love your family, have your friends, and that's basically it."

As spring gave way to summer, Kobe maintained his busy schedule. In fact, he took on even greater responsibilities and challenges. In what little spare time he had, Kobe decided he would try to exercise his mind as well as his body. So he enrolled in a course in advanced Italian at UCLA. At first he found the schoolwork difficult. After all, he hadn't been in a classroom in more than a year, and now he was trying to cram a semester's worth of work into one ten-week summer session. For a while Kobe found it hard to sit still and concentrate. He was accustomed to hard work, but he was not accustomed to working so . . . *quietly.*

"I thought I was gonna die in there the first week," he said. "Then I got used to it again. I had the book bag, the notepad, I was taking notes— the whole thing."

Kobe insisted he got no special treatment from his professor. He was simply a student, trying to learn.

The same was true of his experience on the court. Although many second-year players do not participate in the Summer Pro League, Kobe returned in 1997. His mission, as outlined by the Lakers, was to work on weaknesses in his game. Specifically, he was to work on becoming more of a team player. To the casual observer, Kobe appeared to play brilliantly during the twenty-three-day summer session. He averaged more than 20 points per game and seemed to be in the best shape of his young life.

But the Lakers weren't happy. Without getting specific, Jerry West said that he thought Kobe hadn't played well at all during the summer.

He let it be known that expectations would be higher in the coming season, for Kobe was no longer a rookie. Larry Drew, one of the Lakers' assistant coaches and a former NBA point guard, was far more blunt. After watching Kobe try to take over a game by himself one evening, Drew decided it was time to stop treating the kid so gently. There had been too many fancy moves, too many missed shots, too few passes. It was evident to Drew that Kobe still did not see the big picture. He saw only himself. This angered Drew, who knew from experience that the greatest teams are made up of players who understand their roles. Kobe failed to grasp that concept. Or, worse, he was selfish. Either way, his approach to the game was unacceptable.

So Drew did what he felt was necessary. He confronted his young superstar.

"We exchanged words," Drew told the *Los Angeles Daily News*. "I said some harsh things to him because he was playing like the old Kobe."

Always the diplomat, Kobe would later describe the incident as less of a confrontation than an exchange of ideas: "He just told me to slow it down. Our conversation was, basically: 'Dissect the defense a little bit more and pick your spots.' I think sometimes my aggressiveness, my competitiveness, takes over the game unconsciously. I just want to dominate."

Throughout his first two years in the NBA, his mistakes usually sprang from a combination of inexperience and a desire to make something . . . *anything* . . . happen. He found it difficult to stand around, waiting for a play to develop, waiting for a crack in the defense to appear. Kobe was not the most patient young man; sometimes he was so eager to see results that he made bad decisions.

For example, in addition to lifting weights, running sprints, and playing hours of pickup ball in the offseason, Kobe also began working with a freelance shooting coach, a man who had no affiliation with the Lakers. Now, if there was one area in which Kobe did not need improvement, it was in the mechanics of his jump shot. By the time training camp opened, his form had been dramatically altered. His jump shot, so sweet and natural, so fluid, was now stiff and awkward. As Kobe tossed up brick after brick during the first days of practice, the Lakers' coaches were befuddled. When Kobe explained what had happened, they were at once amused and disappointed.

"I couldn't believe it when I heard he had been working with this guy," Jerry West told the *Philadelphia Inquirer Magazine*. "I said, 'My God, Kobe, why did you do that? You need a shooting coach like I need more gray hairs.'"

In time, Kobe's shooting touch returned, and the hard work he had endured during the offseason months began to pay off. The first indication of his improvement had come in the annual Magic Johnson All-Star Game, a charity event to benefit the United Negro College Fund. The game, played before a crowd of nearly 15,000 at the Forum, featured some of the NBA's best players, including Seattle Supersonics point guard Gary Payton and Penny Hardaway of the Orlando Magic. But it was Kobe Bryant who stole the show by scoring a game-high 35 points.

By the time the Lakers opened their exhibition season, it was obvious that Kobe was not the same player that he had been a year earlier. The changes were both physical and emotional. Kobe was more confident, more relaxed. He still had a lot to prove, but at least he was no longer . . . *The Rookie.* One look at his body was all that was required to see that he was still growing, still maturing, and that he'd been working hard during the off-season. He had grown another inch, to 6-foot–7, and added 10 pounds of muscle. A lean, sculpted 210 pounds, he now looked more like a man, and less like the gangly kid he had been a year earlier. Gone, too, was the bald-headed look so popular in the NBA. In its place was a neatly trimmed afro; he also sported a goatee. The makeover was part of a statement that Kobe was trying to make: *This is the real me. Get used to it.*

"When I came to the Lakers last year, I wanted to get a clean start," he told *The Sporting News.* "But this year, this is me. My parents raised me to be an individual. The key to success at anything, I think, is avoiding peer pressure."

As training camp progressed, Kobe commanded increasing respect from his peers. He was the fittest player on the team, and certainly the most competitive. Every scrimmage to Kobe was like a war. He played as hard as he could whenever he was on the floor, even during the most mundane drills. And at least once a day he would startle his teammates with his ingenuity and quickness. "He amazes me," Nick Van Exel told *The Sporting News*. "I see him every day and he still amazes me."

By the time the exhibition season began, the Lakers knew that Kobe was destined to play more than 15 minutes per game. For a while his dramatic improvement was the Lakers' little secret, but it didn't remain a secret very long. In one of the Lakers' exhibition games, against the Washington Wizards, Kobe threw down a dunk that became a staple of highlight reels for the rest of the year. The move began with a crossover dribble to shake Washington's Jimmy Oliver near the top of the key. When he was just a step over the foul line, he went airborne. But his path was blocked by Washington's Ben Wallace, who had slid over to help out. Undaunted, Kobe cradled the ball in his right hand, soared right over the top of Wallace, and slammed the ball through the basket. Wallace, who had expected to draw a charge, could only look up at Kobe helplessly. His reaction, a mixture of awe and disbelief, was shared by just about everyone else on the court.

"He just flat-out jumped over the guy," Van Exel would later tell CNN/SI. "It was unbelievable."

Unbelievable, but also undeniable. Kobe's play in the pre-season was so impressive that it altered the way many basketball analysts viewed the Lakers. It was generally assumed that L.A. was too young, too inexperienced to mount a serious challenge for the NBA championship. The league's best teams, after all, were the Chicago Bulls and Utah Jazz. The best players on both of those teams were well into their thirties, which seemed to support the argument that while basketball may be a young man's game, experience counts most in the playoffs.

The Lakers were one of the youngest teams in the league. On opening day of the 1997–98 season, Shaq and Van Exel were only 25 years old. Eddie Jones was 26, Robert Horry 27, Corie Blount and Rick Fox 28, and Elden Campbell 29. Derek Fisher was only 23.

Kobe Bryant was 19.

There was, however, no mistaking the talent. The Lakers were loaded. And if Kobe was really prepared to make a breakthrough, as it appeared he might be, then perhaps the Lakers just might be good enough to challenge the NBA's graybeards after all.

Both Kobe and the Lakers demonstrated from the outset that they were not pretenders. On opening night at the Forum, Kobe redeemed himself by coming off the bench to score 23 points as the Lakers trounced the Jazz, 104–87. He struggled in the next two games—scoring a total of only eight points in victories over the Knicks and Kings—but then bounced back with a 25-point performance against the Golden State Warriors. Unfortunately, that victory proved costly, as Kobe sprained his ankle on a hard drive to the basket late in the game.

The injury was severe enough to force Kobe out of the Lakers' lineup. While the team traveled to Dallas, San Antonio, and Houston, he stayed behind in Los Angeles, getting treatment on his ankle and watching the games on television. He found the experience enormously frustrating. Not since the exhibition season prior to his rookie year had Kobe suffered a serious injury. Just as everything was starting to fall into place, he was restricted to being a spectator.

Luckily, Kobe proved to be a quick healer. He played 16 minutes and scored 11 points in a 121–95 win over the Vancouver Grizzlies on November 16 as the Lakers ran their record to 8–0. Then, on November 18, he returned with the Lakers to Salt Lake City and a rematch with the Jazz. Kobe hadn't played at the Delta Center since the final game of the Western Conference semifinals in 1997. More than anyone else on the Lakers, he wanted to win this game. Actually, winning wasn't enough. Kobe had something to prove. Something personal.

"I told him I hoped he would get the last shot to win the game," coach Del Harris remembered. "He said, 'Payback is going to be . . .'"

Kobe didn't finish that thought. He didn't need to. The coach knew exactly what he meant. As it turned out, Kobe did not get a chance to take the game-winning shot, but he did play a major role in the outcome of the game. With four seconds remaining and the Lakers clinging to a 95–92 lead, and the Delta Center crowd in full-throated roar again, Utah's Bryon Russell took the potential game-tying jump shot. Kobe, however, jumped out on Russell and swatted the shot away. As if that wasn't sweet enough, Kobe ran down the loose ball, scooped it up, and cruised in for a backboard-shaking dunk for the last of his 19 points as the final buzzer sounded.

"I made sure I was ready to make a play tonight," Kobe said after the game. "I put a lot of pressure on myself to visualize a game-ending situation. I had to make it happen."

If anyone was happier than Kobe about the way the game ended, it was Del Harris. "He's not a kid anymore," the coach said proudly. "He's an NBA player. Kobe made that clear tonight. The rest of the NBA better watch out for this guy."

The Lakers, too, merited attention. With the victory over the Jazz they improved their record to 9–0, the best start in the history of the franchise. It was, of course, a long season, but in Los Angeles title talk had already begun.

10

AIR APPARENT

The Lakers kept up their torrid pace through most of the first month of the 1997–98 season. On November 23 they ran their record to 11–0 with a 119–102 victory over the Los Angeles Clippers. The Clippers were one of the NBA's lowliest teams, but it was still an important victory, since it was achieved despite the absence of Shaquille O'Neal. Shaq had pulled an abdominal muscle and was expected to be sidelined for only a few games. As it turned out, though, he was lost for several weeks. Shaq is a big fan of boxing, and sometimes he likes to train on a heavy bag to stay in shape, especially when he's not able to play basketball. During one of those sessions in late November, he sustained a hairline fracture in his right wrist. By the time he returned to the Lakers' lineup, it was almost January, and he'd missed 20 consecutive games.

The Lakers could have folded without Shaq.

No one would have been surprised. They were so young and inexperienced that it was hard to imagine they'd be able to compensate easily for the loss of their leading scorer and rebounder. In fact, the winning streak did soon come to an end. On November 25, at Miami, the Lakers were held to their second-lowest point total of the season in a 106–83 loss to the Heat. Over the course of the next two weeks the Lakers lost more games than they won. Their record fell to 15–5.

But even in defeat there were signs that the team was growing, maturing. The most vivid example was the play of Kobe Bryant. With Shaq out of the lineup, Kobe was compelled to take on an expanded offensive role. His playing time increased to more than 25 minutes per game. His scoring increased, too: 19 points against the Philadelphia 76ers, 21 against the Cleveland Cavaliers, and 20 against the Golden State Warriors. L.A. lost all of those games, but the play of Kobe Bryant was cause for optimism. On December 12 he scored 27 points in 26 minutes as the Lakers snapped a three-game losing streak with a 119–102 victory over the Houston Rockets. Two days later Kobe erupted for a career-high 30 points in a 119–89 victory over the Dallas Mavericks. That was just a glimpse of things to come, for on December 17, against the world champion Chicago Bulls, Kobe scored 33 points!

The Bulls were too much for the Shaq-less Lakers that day. They won easily, 104–83, at the United Center in Chicago. Still, it was thrilling to see Kobe match up so effectively against Michael Jordan. For two hours the NBA's reigning king dueled with the young prince. *Air Jordan against the Air Apparent.* Jordan was typically masterful, scoring 36 points on an assortment of dunks, drives, and fadeaway jumpers. But Kobe was impressive, too. On one play he froze Jordan— arguably the NBA's best defender—with a beautiful fake and then breezed in for a dunk.

After the game Kobe was gracious enough, and smart enough, to choose his words carefully. Jordan has a reputation for remembering every insult, every unkind word, and using it as motivation. Kobe had scored 33 points, but Jordan had scored 36. More important, the Bulls had won the game—convincingly. So Kobe politely praised his opponent and admitted that he, and the Lakers, still had a lot to learn. As for Jordan, who is as competitive a player as the NBA has ever known, he couldn't help but be impressed by Kobe's athleticism. "I remember when I had that much energy," he said with a smile.

The amount of fuel in Michael Jordan's tank was a matter of great concern to anyone who cared about the future of professional basketball. It was no secret that the league had risen to its current position as the most popular and successful professional sports league on the planet primarily on the strength of three dynamic personalities: Larry Bird, Magic Johnson, and Michael Jordan. Prior to the arrival of Bird and Magic in 1979, the NBA had struggled to acquire and maintain a widespread following. Bird, with his phenomenal shooting touch and court vision, and Magic, with his dynamic personality and passing ability, changed everything. They captured the imagination of sports fans across the country and helped transform the league into a mainstream product.

A few years later, in 1984, Jordan came along, and suddenly the NBA's popularity soared beyond the boundaries of the United States. There had never been a player quite like Jordan. At the University of North Carolina his spectacular athletic ability was only rarely displayed, since the Tar Heels were locked into a rigid offensive system. Once he reached the NBA, he blossomed. He did things with a basketball that no one had ever done—things no one had ever *seen*. He was only 6-foot–6, but he routinely dunked over players half a foot taller. There seemed to be no limit to his shooting range. He averaged 28.2 points a game in 1984–85 and was named Rookie of the Year. The first of seven straight scoring titles came in 1986–87. By 1990 the Bulls had surrounded Jordan with a strong supporting cast, and were on their way to the first of five NBA championships they would win in the 1990s.

Along the way Jordan became the richest and most recognizable athlete in the world. He earned millions of dollars for playing basketball, and many millions more for endorsing products by Nike, McDonald's, and others. Unlike some athletes, Michael did not allow the money to weaken him. He remained the most competitive player in the NBA. In 1993, when he sensed his desire waning, he sought out a new challenge. At only thirty years of age he shocked the basketball world by announcing his retirement from the NBA. For the next year, in what he described as a desire to fulfill a lifelong dream, he played minor league baseball in the Chicago White Sox organization. Even the great Michael Jordan, though, couldn't switch sports in mid-life. After failing to make it to the major leagues, he returned to the NBA at the end of the 1994–95 season, and in 1996 led the Bulls back to the NBA championship.

During Jordan's absence the NBA experienced a significant loss of interest among its fans. Attendance slipped. Television ratings fell. Clearly, to a certain segment of the population, Michael Jordan was synonymous with basketball. If he wasn't playing, there was no point in watching. So, for the past few years, as Jordan has aged and begun to talk about the inevitability of retirement, the question has repeatedly been asked: Who will carry the torch for the NBA in the next millennium?

Where is the next Michael Jordan?

More and more, as the 1997–98 season progressed, the answer seemed to be: *He's in Los Angeles.*

Comparisons between Kobe and Michael became increasingly common. They were, after all, roughly the same size and blessed with the same otherworldly athleticism. Even their speaking voices were eerily similar: a deep, confident baritone. Like Michael, Kobe was already on the verge of becoming a star of such magnitude that he needed only one name. Like Michael, he was fiercely competitive, even in practice sessions. And, like Michael, he left teammates and opponents alike awestruck by what he could do with the basketball.

"Whew. Kobe Bryant. That's the real deal right there," Denver Nuggets coach Bill Hanzlik told the *Denver Post.* "He's supposed to be—what?—a sophomore in college right now? That's scary. That's real scary . . . Kobe grooves with confidence and ability. He's like a fine wine. You know he's just going to get better."

Dennis Scott, then a forward for the Dallas Mavericks, agreed. "He's one of those special talents," Scott told *USA Today.* "The big fellow [Shaq] is still the leader of that team. They know it, and Kobe knows it. But give him a couple more years and he might be the man of this whole league."

Throughout the league people began jumping on the Kobe Bryant bandwagon. And with good reason. Even after Shaq returned to the Lakers' lineup in January, Kobe continued to be one of the team's most consistently productive players. He played 25 to 30 minutes per game and was the team's third-leading scorer, behind only Shaq and Eddie Jones. His play was hardly flawless. Sometimes he still took bad shots and made poor decisions. But those occasions were less frequent. And at least once each night he did something spectacular—a blinding move to the basket, a no-look pass, a reverse dunk.

"He did a dunk earlier this year, caught it on the break, jumped, and everyone thought he was going to dunk it on one side," teammate Jon Barry told CNN/SI. "He brought it down with two hands and reversed it around the other side, just out of the blue. All of us looked at each other and said, 'Where did that one come from? What's next?'"

Barry also recalled another spectacular dunk, against the Atlanta Hawks. "He gets the ball, goes up for a layup, turns, and there's a guy right there, and he 360s and lays it in. It was so smooth. It wasn't rehearsed. I bet he's never done it before and he just did it. That's what came into his head and that's what his body did. An incredible move and he made it look so easy. A lot of things he does look so easy for him."

A handful of NBA players are so extraordinarily talented and creative that other players routinely say they would pay to watch them play. Jordan has always fallen into that category. In only his second year, at the tender age of nineteen, Kobe was also becoming that type of attraction. Even Vlade Divac, whose unhappy departure from Los Angeles was caused by Kobe's arrival, marveled at the young man's artistry.

"I follow him, not because we were traded for each other, but because I see him as the next Michael Jordan," Divac told *Courtside* magazine. "He has all the potential and all the talent. If you look at him in his second year, it looks like he's already been in the league ten years. He plays with so much confidence. If you didn't know how old he is, it would be normal. But he's a nineteen-year-old kid playing like a thirty-year-old. He's for real."

The people most impressed by Kobe were those closest to him, the players and coaches who saw him on a daily basis. As Eddie Jones told *Courtside*, "He can be the best to ever play this game. He has so much talent. The kid is just incredible."

In an interview with the *Philadelphia Inquirer*, Robert Horry said it wouldn't be long before Kobe would be the focus of the Lakers' offense: "Pretty soon other players will have to fit in around him. Kobe is going to be the best player ever."

Even better than Michael Jordan? a reporter asked Horry.

"Yep. Kobe's got Michael's skills and Michael's will. But Kobe came into the league when he was eighteen, and he's going to accomplish more."

Horry's assessment was logical. In the first half of the 1997–98 season Kobe averaged 17.9 points, 3.3 rebounds, and 2.4 assists while playing 26.7 minutes per game. Those numbers did not compare to Jordan's second year in the NBA. Then again, by the time Jordan completed his second year, he was twenty-three years old. Considering his age and lack of experience, Kobe was playing remarkably well. He was, in fact, the NBA's leading scorer off the bench, and a candidate for Sixth Man of the Year honors.

Kobe's combination of talent, good looks, personality, and youth combined to make him one of the NBA's biggest stars at an age when most kids are still adjusting to college life. The magnitude of his fame wasn't really evident until late January, when rosters for the NBA's annual All-Star Game were announced. As the league's most productive sixth man, Kobe was a candidate to be a reserve for the West squad, since reserves are selected by the league's coaches. The starting lineups for the All-Star Game, however, are chosen by the fans, and they made their affection for Kobe known by making him one of the two leading vote getters (the other was Seattle's Gary Payton) at guard.

So, despite not having started a single game for his own team all season, Kobe Bryant was the youngest starter in NBA All-Star history. The person he replaced in the record books was Magic Johnson, who was a twenty-year-old rookie when he started in his first All-Star Game. Kobe had some fast company on the West squad. In addition to Payton, the starting lineup included Shaquille O'Neal, Utah's Karl Malone, and Minnesota's Kevin Garnett.

"It's definitely cool, [the fans] acknowledging the hard work I did in the off-season and the work I've been doing in the regular season," Kobe said when he heard that he'd been chosen. "It's good to know they support you, that they're out there responding to what you do.

"I'd like to thank all the fans who voted for me and who showed such an interest in the NBA. Last year, when I participated in the slam dunk contest, the whole atmosphere surrounding All-Star Weekend was exciting. This year, to play in the All-Star Game with all the greatest players in the league is going to be a great honor."

After Kobe was named to the All-Star team, the publicity machine kicked into high gear. Newspapers and magazines across the country ran feature stories on Kobe. He appeared on the covers of *Sports Illustrated, Inside Sports,* and

Newsweek. He even appeared on *Meet the Press.*

For Kobe it was a dizzying experience. In two short years he had gone from high school to the top of the NBA food chain. Well, close to the top. Above him still was Michael Jordan. But the gap, it seemed, was narrowing. Not that Kobe really cared.

"That's a great compliment—don't get me wrong—but I'm my own man," he told *Inside Sports.* "People make those comparisons so they can relate to the individual a little bit more. But I can't be worrying about what people are saying around me. I smile and say, 'Thank you very much,' and just keep moving on."

A smart philosophy, especially since not everyone was in Kobe's corner. Some people, like Orlando Magic guard Penny Hardaway, simply weren't buying the hype. "Every year someone else is said to be the next Jordan," Hardaway told *Newsweek.* "I was said to be the next one, and then there was Grant Hill, and don't forget Mr. Baby Jordan, Harold Miner—where is he now? Everyone is always saying this and that, and the minute you hit a rough spot in your game, you're no longer on the road to becoming the next Jordan. That's a lot of pressure."

True, but if anyone was capable of handling that pressure, it was Kobe. A week before the All-Star Game, the Bulls traveled to Los Angeles for a rematch with the Lakers. Again, Jordan won the individual battle, outscoring Kobe,

31–20. This time, though, the Lakers won the game, by a score of 112–87. At the All-Star break they were 34–11, only a half game behind Pacific Division leader Seattle.

The crowd that turned out for the All-Star Game on February 8 at New York's Madison Square Garden included a dazzling array of celebrities. In the front row were actors Jack Nicholson and Leonardo DiCaprio, musicians Madonna and the artist formerly known as Prince, filmmaker Spike Lee, and Magic Johnson. If they had come to see a showdown between the NBA's present and future stars, they weren't disappointed.

Kobe was wired in the opening minutes. In fact, he was so excited that he nearly reverted back to his rookie form, when he sometimes forgot that there were other players on the floor. He touched the ball 11 times in the first quarter. On all but one of those touches, he shot the ball. The very first time the ball came to Kobe, he drove right to the basket, challenging Jordan to stop him. "I had to," Kobe later explained, "or he would have killed me. The only thing he understands is aggressiveness." Fortunately, Kobe happened to have a fairly hot hand. He finished the quarter with eight points, one fewer than Jordan; at halftime, the score was Michael 13, Kobe 10.

"We were trying to get [Kobe] off early," said Eddie Jones, one of four Lakers named to the West squad. "We were trying to get him the ball and let him get going."

In the end, it was Jordan's day, as it so often is. Despite suffering from the flu, the thirty-five-year-old veteran scored 23 points and was named MVP as the East routed the West, 135–114. But the most memorable moments of the day were delivered by the nineteen-year-old newcomer, who led the West with 18 points, despite sitting out the entire fourth quarter. The first highlight came early in the game, when he spun 360 degrees in the air before throwing down a thunderous dunk. Moments later he dunked again, this time off an alley-oop pass from Kevin Garnett. Finally, late in the first half, Kobe improvised one of the most unusual moves in All-Star Game history. While driving to the basket on the right side of the lane, Kobe put the ball behind his back with his left hand, resumed his dribble with the same hand, switched to his right hand, and then threw in a baseline hook shot while falling out of bounds.

The crowd, of course, went wild. Kobe, like a proud artist, just smiled.

He was still smiling in the locker room afterward, the thrill of having played in his first All-Star Game etched on his face. "Can I sum it up?" he said. "Nah. If I could, I would. If you want to know how I'm feeling right now, I'm excited. And I'm a little sad because it's over."

There would, of course, be other All-Star

games. With his performance in New York, Kobe had made certain that his fan club would continue to swell. It now included one very prominent new member. His name was Michael Jordan, and as he walked off the floor at Madison Square Garden, he could be seen throwing an arm around the Air Apparent. "I just told Kobe to keep going and stay strong because there are always expectations and pressures," Jordan later explained in an interview with *Newsweek*. "I know what too much pressure too soon can do to you, and I just wanted him to be aware. But he's a smart kid with a bright future. He'll figure it out."

11

SOPHOMORE SLUMP

The NBA season is among the longest and most grueling in all of professional sports. In addition to the 82-game regular season, which runs from the end of October through the end of April, players must survive training camp, pre-season exhibition games, and, if they're lucky, several weeks of playoff games. For anyone fortunate enough to reach the NBA finals, the season stretches out over nearly ten months.

For even the toughest of veterans, it is an exhausting journey, both physically and emotionally. For those unaccustomed to the rigors of NBA life, it can be thoroughly debilitating. Most rookies have never played more than 35 games in a single season. Suddenly they're asked to double that output. And they're playing against better competition, for much higher stakes. They must adapt to life on the road, which can be a nightmare of its own. Late-night plane trips in stormy weather are common, followed by a few hours of fitful sleep in a strange hotel room. It's not unusual for young players to ignore the warning signs sent by their bodies. They believe they're invincible, that nothing can hurt them. After all, they were stars in college. They were rarely sick or injured. Life was easy.

In the NBA fitness is paramount. Everyone is talented. Everyone is athletic. The player who stays mentally sharp and physically healthy is the one most likely to thrive. A slight ankle sprain in October, if not treated carefully, can have consequences in April. It's understood that when you earn millions of dollars, you'll play with pain once in a while. The trick is to keep those occasions to a minimum. For younger players that can be a problem. Their bodies have not yet adjusted to the harsh reality of NBA life. So they get hurt. Or, more commonly, they hit . . . *The Wall.*

The wall can't be touched or felt, but its existence can't be denied. Just as a marathon runner often crashes into this invisible barrier near the end of a race, so too does a basketball player find himself wearing down in the final months of the season. This peculiar development is most common among rookies who are given substantial playing time. For a while they respond admirably. Young and hungry, they adjust quickly to their new lives. Their play is fueled by equal parts emotion and talent. By the All-Star Break it seems as though the transition from college to the NBA is going to be smooth.

Then the wall rears up.

The first half of the NBA season is longer than the longest college season. So it's not surprising that when March and April roll around, the rookies begin to fade. They've played 50 games . . . 60 games . . . 70 games . . . 80 games! Their knees are begging for mercy. Their backs ache. Their hands are callused and raw. In all likelihood, they're at least 10 pounds lighter than they were at the start of the season. They want to keep playing hard, but they simply can't. For them the season is all but over.

Kobe Bryant did not hit the wall in his rookie year, mainly because he averaged only 15.5 minutes per game. His legs remained fresh, his attitude entirely positive. The second year was a different story. Kobe's growth and improvement proved to be a burden as well as a blessing, for suddenly he was expected to be a far more important member of the team. Although technically the Lakers' sixth man, he was the team's third-leading scorer. He routinely logged more playing time than some of the starters. Although Kobe was now an All-Star whose fame was rapidly surpassing that of some of the league's best players, he was still just nineteen years old. In the history of the NBA, no one had ever made such a dramatic impact at such a young age. But the All-Star Game did not represent the finish line. It was merely the halfway point in a very long journey. Before it was over, Kobe would have his first encounter with the wall.

Just one day after the All-Star Game, coach Del Harris met with the media after a practice session. Not surprisingly, given his performance in New York, much of the conversation centered on Kobe Bryant. It was perfectly reasonable to speculate on Kobe's status. If he was capable of holding his own against Michael Jordan in the All-Star Game, then wasn't he ready to become a starter for the Los Angeles Lakers?

Harris bristled at the suggestion.

"I told reporters all week that Kobe would be terrific in that game," he said. "From the questions they were asking, I think they doubted that he should have been voted in as a starter by the fans. I knew Kobe would meet the challenge. And he did. He's only nineteen, but he's ready to be on that stage.

"But as for our team, Kobe fulfills an important role as our sixth man. He comes in with energy and makes us even stronger. And it's good for him because the opponent doesn't know if he's coming in at forward or guard, and can't set its game plan for him. It won't always be this way, but this is the way it is now."

To his credit, Kobe did not allow the All-Star experience to go to his head. If the Lakers wanted him to continue to provide a spark off the bench, then he would gladly accept that role. "If they're bringing me along at their pace, that's fine," he said. "I just want to win. We have the second best record in the league and I'm playing a lot, so there are no complaints. Of course, if they want me to do more, that'll be good, too."

Interestingly, the very next day Kobe started his first game of the season. He had 17 points and four rebounds while playing 30 minutes in a 117–105 loss to the Trail Blazers. Over the next few weeks Kobe continued to play a vital role for the Lakers. In a 113–108 loss to Seattle, he scored 15 points while playing a season-high 41 minutes. On February 19 he scored 21 points in 35 minutes as the Lakers rolled past the Denver Nuggets, 131–92. Three nights later he had 18 points in 37 minutes against the Orlando Magic. During the month of February, Kobe averaged 15.6 points and nearly 30 minutes per game. With each successive appearance he seemed to be getting more comfortable. His play was marked by confidence and intelligence.

As February gave way to March, however, Kobe began to struggle. In the longest, hardest stretch of the season—the dog days between the All-Star Break and the stretch run to the play-offs—Kobe fell into the worst slump of his basketball career.

It began with a one-for-eight shooting performance on February 25 against the Indiana

Pacers, and escalated during a 101–89 loss to the Knicks on March 1 at Madison Square Garden. This was Kobe's first trip to New York since All-Star Weekend, when he was a media darling and fan favorite. But there was no outpouring of support on this occasion. With its raucous, knowledgeable fans, the Garden is one of the toughest places in the NBA for a team to win. Although one young fan carried a sign saying "Kobe, will U marry me after you move out of your mom's house?" the Garden crowd generally treated Kobe like the enemy that day. They howled each time he missed a shot and cheered each time he made a mistake. When he blew a dunk late in the game, the crowd began chanting sarcastically, "Ko-be! Ko-be!"

He finished with a respectable 14 points, but he was clearly unhappy with the way he played. He made just four of 15 field goal attempts. "I'm ticked at myself," he said. "I'm not doing a good job as far as benefitting the team goes. I don't like the way I'm playing. I'm very, very upset."

Del Harris pointed out that Kobe's troubles were at least partially due to the fact that he was no longer being overlooked by opponents. On many nights he was the center of attention. For the first time in his professional career he was feeling the effects of being marked carefully all over the floor. He was discovering what it was like to be double-teamed. "It used to be that I'd get by one guy and I'd be home free," Kobe said.

"But now there's always a second guy there. It's like a chess game."

And Kobe was no grand master—at least not yet. His downward spiral continued for several weeks. On March 2, during a 96–86 loss to the Washington Wizards, he scored four points while playing just 12 minutes. The Lakers then went on a six-game winning streak, but Kobe's contributions were limited. As he had been a year earlier, Del Harris was faced with a difficult decision: allow the future superstar to play his way out of the slump, or cut back on his minutes. The coach chose the latter option. In March, Kobe suffered through several disappointing nights. He played only 12 minutes and scored just six points in a 108–85 victory over the Clippers. In a 101–89 loss to the Supersonics on March 16, he played 14 minutes, took just one shot, and, for the first time all season, failed to score. Three nights later, against the Phoenix Suns, Kobe played 28 minutes. It was the most court time he had logged in nearly a month. Unfortunately, his jump shot was still missing in action. He made just one of 10 field goal attempts.

For Kobe, and the Lakers, one of the lowest points of the season came on March 28 at the Delta Center in Salt Lake City, Utah. In what many people considered to be a preview of the Western Conference championship, the Jazz handled the Lakers, 106–91. The game was intensely emotional for both teams. Near the end, Jazz forward Greg Foster threw down a dunk on a breakaway and then celebrated by thumping his chest and drawing a finger across his throat in a slicing motion, implying that the Lakers were dead. The crowd loved it. The Lakers did not. Harris leaped off the bench and berated one of the referees, demanding that Foster be given a technical foul for taunting. But it was Harris who ended up getting hit with a technical. After the game, Shaquille O'Neal promised that neither he nor the Lakers would forget Foster's showboating.

"Foster's just a fake, that's all," Shaq said. "He's a fake—f-a-k-e. Certain guys get on certain teams with great players, and they think they're great. Foster is a bum. He's just hiding behind [Jeff] Hornacek and Stockton. He's a bum, period. The next time he goes up, he better go up strong, because a couple guys might try to take his head off. It's okay to have emotion, but what goes around, comes around."

For Kobe, things couldn't get much worse. Or could they? Just three days after being held to two points and zero rebounds against the Jazz, he scored 17 points in a victory over the Toronto Raptors. It was one of the better games Kobe had played in some time. He made seven of 13 shots—including two of four from three-point range—and had five assists. But just as his game was starting to come back, his health deteriorated. Late in the third quarter he began to feel a sharp pain in his abdomen. By the start of the fourth quarter he was in the locker room.

The injury, a jammed pelvis, turned out to be annoying but not serious. The Lakers were in the final month of their season now, and Kobe, like everyone else, would have to adjust to playing with a little discomfort. That didn't bother him. He was more concerned with recapturing the form that had made him the league's best sixth man in the first half of the season.

Slowly, steadily, he was able to do precisely that. On April 2, in a 117–106 victory over the New Jersey Nets, Kobe made seven of 11 shots and scored 20 points. His performance was over-shadowed by a remarkable 50-point effort from Shaquille O'Neal, but it was encouraging nonetheless. With Shaq playing his best basket-ball of the season, and Kobe emerging from his slump, the Lakers were once again looking like a team with championship aspirations. As Kobe said, "I think everybody's pumped for the play-offs."

Over the last three weeks of the season, the Lakers were the hottest team in the NBA. They were healthier than they had been all season, and they had settled on a consistent, productive rota-tion. As they approached the playoffs, the starters were Derek Fisher at point guard, Eddie

Jones at shooting guard, Rick Fox and Robert Horry at forward, and Shaquille O'Neal at center. Fisher had stepped in while Van Exel was recovering from a knee injury, and even though Van Exel was perfectly healthy by the end of the season, Harris decided to stick with Fisher. With Van Exel and Kobe as their top reserves, the Lakers now had the most explosive bench in the league.

The Lakers won their first four games in April before losing to the Phoenix Suns, 114–105. But they rebounded quickly from that setback, reeling off victories over the Golden State Warriors, San Antonio Spurs, and Dallas Mavericks. On the final day of the regular season they met the Utah Jazz at the Great Western Forum. The game had only mild playoff implications. The Jazz had the best record in the NBA and were already assured of home-court advantage throughout the playoffs. The Lakers, meanwhile, were still hoping to win the Pacific Division title. In order to finish first, they had to beat the Jazz and hope that Seattle lost to Portland in its final game. It was, for the Lakers, a long shot. More important was that they play well against the league's best team—a team they would probably have to beat in the playoffs if they were going to win the NBA championship. After playing so poorly in their last meeting with the Jazz, the Lakers needed to make a statement.

And that's exactly what they did. They beat

the Jazz by a score of 102–98 to take the season series, 3–1. They won because Shaq was a monstrous presence inside, scoring 35 points and grabbing 15 rebounds. But they also won because Kobe Bryant played one of his best games. In 37 minutes Kobe hit 10 of 19 shots and scored 25 points. He was at his best in the fourth quarter, when the Lakers needed him most. Kobe's two free throws tied the score at 83–83, and his impressive dunk with 7:03 left in the game put the Lakers ahead for good, 85–83. The Jazz were still within striking range with 1:24 to play, when a free throw by Utah's Bryon Russell made it 93–90. But Kobe came up with the biggest play of the day with 1:01 remaining, nailing a long three-pointer as the 24-second clock expired to put the game out of reach.

Not long after the game ended, the Lakers found out that the Sonics had beaten the Trail Blazers. The Lakers and Sonics finished with identical 61–21 records, but Seattle earned the Pacific Division title by winning the head-to-head series with Los Angeles.

For the Lakers, it was a bittersweet conclusion to the regular season. Despite winning 22 of their last 25 games, they would have to settle for being the number three seed in the Western Conference playoffs. Still, as Shaq said, "We wanted to come out and end the season on a positive note. We did what we were supposed to do today."

They all did their jobs, especially Kobe. In the last four games of the regular season he averaged 19 points and nearly 30 minutes per game. Best of all, he made 54 percent of his field-goal attempts. Of all of Kobe's accomplishments, perhaps none was more impressive than this: he had fought his way out of the first prolonged slump of his young life. He had run into the wall . . . and survived.

12

SHOWTIME!

In the days leading up to the 1998 NBA play-offs, there was a lot of speculation about Kobe Bryant and his ability to play under pressure. Almost a full year had passed since the night in Salt Lake City when he tossed up four air balls in the Lakers' season-ending loss to the Utah Jazz. He had been an eighteen-year-old rookie then, one of the youngest players in the history of the league. That he would have difficulty adjusting to the tension and intensity of playoff basketball was understandable. But Kobe was a year older now. He was far more experienced and clearly a better basketball player.

There were expectations now. Kobe was the third-leading scorer on one of the best teams in the NBA. He had endured a roller coaster of a season, but if the Lakers were going to make a serious run at a championship, they would need a strong and confident Kobe Bryant. They did not need a player who was worried about repeating the mistakes he had made a year earlier. Fortunately, it wasn't Kobe's nature to fret. As awful as the experience in Utah had been, Kobe said, it had only made him stronger. He was eager for another taste of playoff basketball.

"I think I've just improved as a basketball player," he said. "I worked very hard in the off-season and learned a lot playing last year, a lot of experiences. So, for the playoffs, this year I'll be more prepared."

Among the observers who agreed with that assessment was Kobe's boyhood idol, Magic Johnson. "Kobe will be one of the best clutch players in NBA history," Johnson told the *Los Angeles Daily News.* "He wants it. He has no fear about whether he's the goat or not. That's what a clutch player has got to do. You take all that weight on and say, 'Well, if I miss it, I can deal with that.' Most of the time, in your head, you think you can make every shot. You can tell by his play now, he thinks he can make every shot. He just has to mature and realize what's a good shot and what's not a good shot. But I would love to have him in a year or two because . . . watch out!"

As the Lakers' first-round series with the Portland Trail Blazers drew near, Kobe's confidence became less of an issue than his health. Back spasms forced him to miss two practice sessions, and rumors circulated that Kobe might miss the opening game. As Kobe emerged from a session with Lakers strength and conditioning coach Jim Cotta on the eve of the playoffs, though, he declared himself fit and ready for competition. "I'll be okay," he said. "Tomorrow, my adrenaline will be going strong, and everything will be moving so fast, I don't think I'll have time to think about my back."

The first round of the NBA playoffs is a best-of-five format: the first team to win three games advances to the second round. Game one of the Portland-LA series was played April 24 at the Great Western Forum. For Kobe the game reflected the type of season he had experienced: at times he played like a nineteen-year-old kid; at other times he played like an all-star. As for the Lakers, well, they did not exactly look like the hottest team in basketball. Early in the third quarter, in fact, the Trail Blazers held a 58–47 lead. As the fourth quarter began, the game was tied, 74–74.

Then Kobe came to life. He scored 11 of his 15 points in the final nine minutes to help the Lakers post a 104–102 victory. He made three of four field goals and four of seven free throws in the fourth quarter. As he had been a year earlier against the Jazz, he was asked to play a vital role down the stretch. And this time he handled the responsibility like a seasoned pro.

"I'm not going to lie and say it didn't cross my mind, because it did cross my mind," Kobe told reporters afterward. "But also all the close games that we had this past season. I tried to recall those games that I came through for us, whether on the free-throw line or a rebound or a shot. That kind of gets your confidence going.

"I wanted to be successful in the fourth quarter. I wanted to come out with a good fourth quarter because I wanted to win the basketball game. So after the buzzer went off and we had a two-point lead, I was like, 'Aahh. Good job, man. Good job. Now you can sleep tonight.'"

The Lakers won Game 2 by a score of 108–99, despite getting only four points from Kobe. The series then shifted to Portland for Game 3, where the Trail Blazers played with much greater confidence. Led by point guard Damon Stoudamire's 18 points, the Blazers beat the Lakers, 99–94, to avoid an embarrassing first-round sweep. They were able to stay alive primarily because they limited Shaq to 19 points, and because Kobe had a disappointing game. He played only 16 minutes and made just one of six shots from the field. For the second consecutive game he finished with four points, far below his season average.

In Game 4, the Lakers looked like the team they had been in the final month of the season— a slick, aggressive team with extraordinary offensive firepower. Playing with intensity and focus from the opening tip, the Lakers outscored the Trail Blazers 16–1 during one memorable stretch early in the game. Shaq led the attack, scoring

13 of his game-high 31 points in the first period as L.A. opened up a 28–19 lead and breezed to a 110–99 victory.

Kobe, meanwhile, reverted to All-Star form. His thunderous dunk with 4:19 left in the game gave the Lakers a 94–74 lead, their biggest advantage of the afternoon. But there was more to Kobe's performance than the usual highlight-reel acrobatics. In what was easily the best play-off game of his career, Kobe had 22 points, four assists, and three rebounds in 36 minutes. He made nine of 16 shots from the field and exhibited not only a flair for the dramatic, but the patience and intelligence of a veteran player.

Afterward, Kobe was reluctant to discuss his own performance. Like the rest of the Lakers, he was trying to concentrate on the bigger picture. "Everybody's intensity was higher tonight," he said. "We were pumped up for Game 3, but tonight our adrenaline was pumping and we got it done. We're taking it a game at a time, and that's what our focus needs to be."

The Lakers expected a much more formidable challenge in the Western Conference semifinals, where their opponent would be the Seattle Supersonics. Deep and experienced, the Sonics were perennial title contenders. They had perhaps the NBA's best point guard in Gary Payton and one of the top front-court players in 6–11

Vin Baker. They also had George Karl, one of the league's most successful coaches, on the bench.

As the Pacific Division champions, Seattle had home-court advantage in the best-of-seven series. The Lakers knew it was important that they play well in Game 1. They had to play fearlessly in the opening minutes if they were to have any hope of taking the notoriously vocal crowd at KeyArena out of the game. A good performance in Game 1 would support the contention that the Lakers were more than just a talented young team; they were serious about winning a championship. A poor performance, on the other hand, might stamp them as pretenders.

As it turned out, the Lakers opened the series with one of their worst games. They were sluggish and sloppy in a 106–92 loss. Kobe played just 16 minutes, hit only one shot from the field, and finished with four points. The next day, after practice, he admitted to feeling somewhat frustrated. It takes time to grow up in the NBA. Kobe knew he still had a lot to learn.

"The hardest part is that everybody is telling me to be patient," he said. "But it's hard for me. I want to go out there and I want to take over. I want to go at Gary [Payton]. I want him to come back at me. That's the hard part."

It wasn't really the *hardest* part, though. As Kobe would soon discover, there is something even worse than playing a limited amount of time. And that's not playing at all.

A few hours after practice on Tuesday, May 5, Kobe began to feel ill. In the middle of the night he became sick to his stomach, and by the next day he was reeling from the effects of a full-blown case of the flu. His body ached. His head was pounding. He had a fever. He couldn't keep any food or water down, so he became dehydrated. Kobe skipped the Lakers' shoot-around on the morning of Game 2 and tried to rest in his hotel room. That evening, as tip-off drew near, he took fluids intravenously in the trainer's room at KeyArena, hoping to gather enough strength to at least make a contribution. But there was no chance.

"You know he would play if he could possibly play at all," Lakers coach Del Harris said. "If the decision were left up to him, I could tell you we couldn't keep him out of the game. But that's why we have medical people."

The scenario was not ideal for the Lakers. It was bad enough that they were trailing in the series and coming off a dismal performance. Now they were going to have to take the floor without their third-leading scorer and most electrifying bench player. Somehow, though, the Lakers responded courageously to the challenge. Eddie Jones picked up the offensive slack by scoring 23 points, and the Lakers as a team were sensational on defense. They defeated the Sonics by a score of 92–68 to even the series at one game apiece.

Two days later, on May 8, the series resumed in Los Angeles. Kobe, unfortunately, was still suffering from the flu and again was forced to be no more than a spectator. And again the Lakers went out and throttled the Sonics, this time by a score of 119–103. Eddie Jones was again spectacular, hitting 19 of 30 shots and scoring 29 points. In the wake of two such convincing victories, both achieved with Kobe on the sideline, there was much debate about whether the Lakers really needed their young superstar all that much. Some people even went so far as to suggest that the team might be better off without Kobe. Seattle forward Sam Perkins, for example, had this to say after Game 3: "Kobe? Oh, him. They don't even miss him. It seems like they're more at ease without him."

The Lakers were quick to dismiss such talk. "Everybody knows at times when Kobe comes into the game, he has the ability to take the game over," said point guard Derek Fisher. "But sometimes he gets into a rush, and sometimes that hurts us. That's the part that everyone has focused on. If we're fortunate enough to move to the next series, Kobe will be an important player for us. We definitely want him back."

Added Robert Horry: "With Kobe out of the game, that's one less piece of firepower that you have. We really need him to get well and get back in."

Kobe was indeed back in the lineup for

Game 4, but he wasn't fully recovered. In fact, he made only a cameo appearance. He played just three minutes and did not attempt a shot. "He was huffing and puffing, as one would expect," said Del Harris. "But it helped. I actually needed him those minutes, and he did a good job." Despite a limited contribution from Kobe, the Lakers continued their winning ways. Thanks in large part to a dominant performance by Shaq, who had 39 points, eight rebounds, seven assists, and five blocked shots, they rolled to their third consecutive victory over the Sonics, 112–102.

Kobe was expected to be at full strength for Game 5, which would be played in Seattle. Harris was eager to have his prodigy back, but he admitted to being slightly concerned about how Kobe would react. After all, Kobe read the newspapers, too. He knew what the Sonics had said about him. Perhaps, the coach admitted, Kobe would be a bit too anxious to prove the Sonics wrong. "It's possible," Harris said. "His tendency is to want to *do* anyway. His normal responses are very aggressive, overt. But he's a very intelligent young man. I'm sure he'll try to be his aggressive self, but he has been working at becoming a player who fits more into the flow of our team."

Kobe gave the Lakers 11 solid minutes in Game 5. He took only three shots and made each one of them. He didn't play much, but he played with intensity and intelligence, and he helped the Lakers eliminate the Sonics, 110–95. Afterward, Kobe promised that he would never forget the Sonics' insults. "I'll be playing against Seattle for many, many years," he said. "I'm just going to have to gun them down the rest of my career."

For the Lakers it was an impressive conclusion to a stunning series. No one had expected them to so thoroughly dominate the Sonics. Seattle, after all, had been one of the most successful franchises in the league in the 1990s. In George Karl's six and a half seasons as head coach, the team had *never* lost four consecutive games.

But the Lakers were hot. Shaq played some of the best basketball of his career against Seattle. He averaged 30.6 points and 9.6 rebounds. He also blocked 20 shots. Early in the series Shaq had exchanged insults with George Karl. By the time the series was over, though, the Seattle coach had nothing but praise for the Lakers' big man. He even went so far as to compare Shaq favorably with one of the greatest centers in NBA history. "Us coaches were talking about Shaq," Karl said. "[Seattle assistant coach] Bob Weiss played against Wilt Chamberlain. He thinks Shaq is better than Wilt, and I agree with him."

Although they were happy, the Lakers celebrated mildly rather than wildly after bumping the Sonics out of the playoffs. That's because their work was far from complete. If they were to reach the NBA finals, they would first have to clear another hurdle. And this one was a bit more formidable. You see, waiting in the Western Conference finals was an old and familiar nemesis.

The Utah Jazz.

"Old" was precisely the word many people had been using to describe the Jazz. Each of their opponents in the first two rounds of the playoffs had enjoyed at least some success against the Jazz. At times, in fact, Utah had looked painfully slow and tired. Their three best players were point guard John Stockton, who was thirty-six years old; power forward Karl Malone, thirty-five; and shooting guard Jeff Hornacek, also thirty-five. Perhaps, after so many seasons with essentially the same lineup, they were finally over the hill.

That, at least, is what Lakers fans wanted to believe. And their sentiments were echoed by various NBA "experts" prior to the Western Conference finals. The Lakers had looked almost unbeatable against Seattle. They were sleek and slick and oozing confidence. If they played as well as they were capable of playing, they would surely have no trouble with the old men from Utah.

Unfortunately, the Lakers who showed up for Game 1 of the Western Conference finals were not the same ones who routed the Sonics.

And the Jazz looked neither old nor slow. In fact, it was Utah that played with more spirit and enthusiasm. With the Delta Center crowd roaring from the opening tip, the Jazz ran away from the Lakers. They opened up a 30-point lead in the first half and cruised to a 112–77 victory.

Afterward, the Lakers seemed stunned. Kobe Bryant couldn't believe that his team had been so thoroughly outplayed by a bunch of guys nearly twice his age. It was, for Kobe, another valuable lesson. "They came out with a lot of energy, and I think it kind of caught us off guard," he said. "We didn't expect such a veteran team to come out with so much energy at the beginning of the game."

It was an embarrassing performance—the worst playoff defeat in Lakers history. The only comparable loss had come in 1985, when the Boston Celtics hammered the Lakers by a score of 148–114 in Game 1 of the NBA finals. That game, played at Boston Garden, was referred to as "The Boston Massacre." The Lakers could only hope that history might repeat itself. Back then, with Magic Johnson leading the way, they rebounded from that terrible start and went on to eliminate the Celtics in six games.

"Yeah, we came in at half-time and everyone was talking about the Boston Massacre," said Kobe. "This is only one game, and we're going to have to forget about it. It's a long series, and we just have to move on."

Kobe had 16 points and four rebounds in Game 1. He was one of the few Lakers who didn't seem to be playing in slow motion. But he would have to play even better if the Lakers were to keep their title hopes alive. And he would need lots of help.

As it happened, the Lakers improved dramatically in Game 2. Shaq had 31 points and Eddie Jones had 19—all in the second half. Kobe added nine points in 22 minutes. The Lakers played tough defense and kept the game close. In the end, though, the Jazz were again the superior team. With Stockton and Malone repeatedly executing one of the oldest plays in basketball—the pick and roll—the Jazz held off the Lakers, 99–95, to take a 2–0 lead in the series.

The Lakers were frustrated by the loss, but with Games 3 and 4 in Los Angeles, they knew the series was far from over. The key, according to Kobe, was not to panic. That had been a problem in the playoffs a year earlier, when they also had lost the first two games in Utah. "Last year we kind of rushed things a little bit, said, 'We have to get these two [wins at home] or else we're packing it up,'" Kobe explained. "That's a natural tendency. But I think experience has taught us not to do that, because that's when you really hurt yourself."

Game 3 was played May 22 at the Great Western Forum. It was a typically star-studded Hollywood crowd. But the Lakers gave them little reason to cheer. Despite a 39-point, 15-rebound effort by Shaq, the Lakers fell to the Jazz for the third consecutive game, 109–98. Afterward, Lakers guard Nick Van Exel seemed to speak for the entire team when he said, "I don't have a clue how to beat these guys."

Like most of his teammates, Kobe struggled in Game 3. He took only four shots and scored nine points. As usual, though, he was upbeat even in defeat. No team had ever come back from a 3–0 deficit in the NBA playoffs. Maybe, Kobe said, the Lakers would be the first. "We're just going to have to come out and play hard," he said. "We're going to have to let it all hang out. It would hurt if we got swept, definitely. We'd definitely be upset. We're upset now. We're in a hole, but we also have an opportunity. There's a first time for everything. This series is definitely not over."

Soon, however, it would be.

Game 4 was played Sunday, May 24, on a brilliant Southern California afternoon. Once again the Forum was sold out. The crowd, proudly imitating the raucous fans in Salt Lake City, did everything it could to energize the Lakers. Shaq once again was unstoppable. He scored 38 points, including 19 in the fourth quarter, as the Lakers fought valiantly to extend the series. As it had throughout the series, though, poor shooting plagued the Lakers. They made just 19 of 57 shots in the first three quarters. During one stretch in the first half, they went six minutes without scoring a single point. As a result, they were forced to play catch-up against a Jazz team that was far too experienced to let the game get away.

Playing like the smartest team in the NBA, the Jazz kept the ball in the right hands down the stretch. Their wisest and most accomplished players, Stockton and Malone, kept marching to the foul line, calmly drilling shot after shot against a backdrop of hysterical Lakers fans.

Each player made six consecutive free throws late in the game, and that proved to be the difference. When the final buzzer sounded, the Jazz walked off the Forum floor with a 96–92 victory and an impressive 4–0 sweep. For them the playoffs would continue. There would be a rematch in the NBA finals with Michael Jordan and the Chicago Bulls. And a chance for an NBA title.

For Kobe Bryant and the Lakers, there was nothing left to do but clean out the lockers. A brilliant season had ended in disappointment. Less than two weeks earlier the Lakers had been the hottest team in basketball. Now they were just litter on the landscape. Like twenty-seven other teams, they would be watching the NBA finals at home.

It was not exactly the ending Kobe Bryant had envisioned. But one of the things that makes Kobe unique is that he is a true student of the game. He planned to draw strength from this experience. Eventually the pain and embarrassment would subside, and he would be a better player for having endured it. Even in defeat, he was studying . . . absorbing . . . growing.

"Obviously, they're an older team that knows a lot more about basketball," Kobe said of the Jazz. "You just try to learn from them. You see Stockton and those guys and you just pick up their tricks."

In a few hours, of course, Kobe would be back out on the floor, practicing what he had learned in some quiet, lonely gym. One season was over, but another had already begun. As Kobe knows, greatness is developed in the shadows, when no one is watching.

STATISTICS

Year	Games	MPG	FG%	3P%	FT%	RPG	APG	PPG
1996-97	71	15.5	.417	.375	.819	1.9	1.4	7.6
1997-98	79	26.0	.428	.341	.794	3.1	2.5	15.4
Career	150	21.1	.425	.354	.801	2.5	1.9	11.7
Playoffs	20	17.7	.397	.243	.760	1.6	1.4	8.5
All Star	1	22.0	.438	.667	1.000	6.0	1.0	18.0

SINGLE-GAME CAREER HIGHS

Points	33
Field Goals Made	12
Field Goals Attempted	21
Three-Point FG Made	4
Three-Point FG Attempted	7
Free Throws Made	13
Free Throws Attempted	14
Offensive Rebounds	4
Total Rebounds	8
Assists	7
Steals	4
Defensive Rebounds	6
Blocks	3
Minutes Played	43

HONORS

- Voted to starting lineup in 1998 NBA All-Star Game

- Youngest All-Star in NBA history

- Named to 1996-97 NBA All-Rookie Second Team

- Winner of 1997 NBA Slam Dunk Championship

- Set single-game scoring record (31 points) in Rookie Game at 1997 NBA All-Star Weekend

- Set record for youngest player ever to appear in an NBA game

- Named 1995-96 National High School Player of the Year by *USA Today* and *Parade*

- Led Lower Merion High School to Pennsylvania Class AAAA state championship

- All-time leading scorer in Southeastern Pennsylvania (2,883 points)

ABOUT THE AUTHOR

A former newspaper columnist and editor, **JOE LAYDEN** has written more than twenty books for children and adults. He is the author of *America on Wheels: The First 100 Years,* a companion piece to the critically acclaimed PBS miniseries on the history of the American automobile; *All the Rage: The Life of an NFL Renegade,* a collaboration with former Dallas Cowboys All-Pro defensive end Charles Haley; *Women in Sports: The Complete Book on the World's Greatest Female Athletes; NBA Game Day; Return of a Champion: The Monica Seles Story;* and *The Art of Magic,* a companion volume to a PBS documentary on the evolution of magic.

Mr. Layden has authored a series of children's sports books for Scholastic, Inc., and is a frequent contributor to *React* magazine. He also presents writing workshops in public and private schools. His work has been honored by the New York Newspaper Publishers Association, the National Associated Press Sports Editors, and the New York State Associated Press Association.

Mr. Layden lives in upstate New York, with his wife, Susan, and their daughter, Emily.